Advance Praise for
The No-Cry Picky Eater Solution

"In *The No-Cry Picky Eater Solution* Elizabeth Pantley provides a whole new way of looking at the age-old problem of what to do when your child's food choices aren't in line with your values. Myths are dispelled by sound, practical, and gentle advice that can work for any family. Old-fashioned thoughts about food battles are challenged, and the solutions are simple and don't involve you becoming a short-order cook. The book was so good, I finished it in one sitting! It was just what I needed for help with my own daughter."

> —Robin Elise Weiss, LCCE, *mother of eight and author of many books for parents, including* The Complete Illustrated Pregnancy Companion, *http://pregnancy.about.com*

"A most supportive and calming spirit, Elizabeth Pantley has once again penned a brilliant guide for parents on a common childhood theme. With savvy tips and tricks to usher our kids into the joys of eating, *The No-Cry Picky Eater Solution* is a sanity saver!"

> —Christine Louise Hohlbaum, *author of* The Power of Slow: 101 Ways to Save Time in Our 24/7 World, *http://powerofslow.wordpress.com*

"Elizabeth Pantley has done it again. Her gentle, respectful approach to parental problem solving shines in tackling this common parenting challenge. Like a strong, calming hand on the shoulder, *The No-Cry Picky Eater Solution* eases parents' fears and provides practical, simple solutions that really work."

> —Stephanie Gallagher, *Cooking for Kids Guide on About.com, http://kidscooking.about.com; and online cooking show host,* The Iron Chef Mom, *http://www.theironchefmom.com*

"Eating is so basic that having a child who is a picky eater can come as a shock to parents. Turning to Elizabeth Pantley's book will help reassure them that their child is typical and healthy, that they are not bad parents, and that there are answers. Elizabeth's approach is respectful of both parents and children, and her book is packed with information and tips. All parents of picky eaters will be encouraged and have a plan once they read this book."

—Kathy Lynn, president, Parenting Today,
http://www.parentingtoday.ca

"This book will put the 'super' back into suppertime—no battles, few leftovers, and lots of table-time connection between parents, caregivers, and kids!"

—Judy Arnall, bestselling author of
Discipline Without Distress: 135 Tools for
Raising Caring, Responsible Children Without
Time-Out, Spanking, Punishment, or Bribery,
www.professionalparenting.ca

"As a mother of four children, I've experienced every kind of eater in my house. The tips and ideas in The No-Cry Picky Eater Solution will enable moms, dads, and caregivers to lay the foundation for healthy, happy eating habits in children that will last a lifetime."

—Maria Bailey, CEO of BSM Media, author, and
Mom Talk Radio host

the no-cry picky eater solution

Gentle Ways to Encourage Your Child to Eat—and Eat Healthy

Elizabeth Pantley

New York Chicago San Francisco Lisbon London Madrid Mexico City
Milan New Delhi San Juan Seoul Singapore Sydney Toronto

1 2 3 4 5 6 7 8 9 10 11 12 13 14 15   QFR/QFR   1 9 8 7 6 5 4 3 2 1

ISBN   978-0-07-174436-2
MHID   0-07-174436-3

e-ISBN   978-0-07-174444-7
e-MHID   0-07-174444-4

This book provides a variety of ideas and suggestions. It is sold with the understanding that the publisher and author are not rendering psychological, medical, or professional services. The author is not a doctor or psychologist, and the information in this book is the author's opinion, unless otherwise stated. This material is presented without any warranty or guarantee of any kind, express or implied, including but not limited to implied warranties of merchantability or fitness for a particular purpose. It is not possible to cover every eventuality in any book, and the reader should consult a professional for individual needs. Readers should bring their child to a medical care provider for regular checkups and bring questions they have to a medical professional or a nutritionist. This book is not a substitute for competent professional health care or professional counseling.

Library of Congress Cataloging-in-Publication Data

Pantley, Elizabeth.
    The no-cry picky eater solution : gentle ways to encourage your child to eat—and eat healthy / by Elizabeth Pantley.
        p.   cm.
    Includes index.
    ISBN-13: 978-0-07-174436-2 (alk. paper)
    ISBN-10: 0-07-174436-3 (alk. paper)
    1. Children—Nutrition.   2. Food preferences in children.   3. Children—Nutrition—Psychological aspects.   I. Title.

    RJ206.P33   2012
    618.92—dc23   2011023407

Credits for the recipes in Part 4 can be found on pages 179–180, which is to be considered an extension of this copyright page.

McGraw-Hill books are available at special quantity discounts to use as premiums and sales promotions or for use in corporate training programs. To contact a representative, please e-mail us at bulksales@mcgraw-hill.com.

This book is printed on acid-free paper.

This book is dedicated to my extraordinary, energetic, and supremely supportive literary agent, Meredith Bernstein, in honor of our work together: ten books, twenty-six languages, countless publicity events, and—most enjoyable—those cherished times we cross the continent to enjoy dinner together. Meredith, thank you for everything. You're the best agent an author could hope for.

Contents

Foreword

Sometime tonight a family will gather around a dinner table. Parents and kids alike will have had a long, busy day, and this will likely be their first moment to sit down together without someone having to dash off somewhere, without phones beeping and televisions blaring. The plates will be set in front of everyone, and as Mom lifts her fork, she notices that her kids are scowling. Few things can cause as much daily strife as raising a picky eater. Before I developed the strategies found in my *Sneaky Chef* books, I too waged a nightly battle with my kids. I wanted them to eat healthy meals so they could be strong and energetic. I wanted to teach them the fundamentals of good eating, so they'd make smart choices throughout their lives. I wanted to be able to make the most of our dinnertime together. I wanted to fix only *one* meal that the entire family would eat. But most of all, I wanted peace. Sound familiar?

The good news is that you don't have to wave the white flag and give in to a lifetime of serving pasta and butter, chicken fingers, bread, or whatever items are on your child's exceedingly small list of "approved" foods. As I've discovered and witnessed in my own and my readers' kitchens, there are plenty of ways to win over even the most finicky eaters. Elizabeth Pantley—and the book you're holding right now—will help you do just that.

The No-Cry Picky Eater Solution provides you with easy-to-follow guidelines on how to talk to your children about healthier eating without provoking clamped mouths, stomped feet, and uneaten dinners. The "fundamental four" are essential for setting your child on the right path to a lifetime of sound eating habits: You need to lead by example; create an environment that mirrors your goals; know proper serving sizes; and remember that all rules shouldn't be rigid, because, hey, we live in the real world. It's simple and doable, and it works.

Elizabeth has a smart understanding of how kids think, what motivates them, and what will scare them away from healthy foods. Employ her practical, helpful suggestions and your family meals will soon become your favorite time of day.

—Missy Chase Lapine
The Sneaky Chef

Missy Chase Lapine is best known as the creator of the wildly successful *Sneaky Chef* series of books, including her first, a *New York Times* bestseller, *The Sneaky Chef: Simple Strategies for Hiding Healthy Foods in Kids' Favorite Meals*. Her methods have not only inspired families around the country but also established a whole new healthy eating and lifestyle brand category. Missy is a member of *Parenting Magazine*'s team of experts, has been a cooking instructor at New York's finest culinary schools, and also serves on the Family Advisory Council of NewYork-Presbyterian Morgan Stanley Children's Hospital, where Sneaky Chef recipes are served to patients. Sneaky Chef's exclusive prepared foods are also featured and sold at select Whole Foods Markets. Visit her at http://www.thesneakychef.com.

Acknowledgments

I would like to express my appreciation to the many people who provide me with their support every day in so many ways:

Meredith Bernstein, of The Meredith Bernstein Literary Agency: counselor, friend, and extraordinary literary agent.

The entire amazing team of people at McGraw-Hill who help me to create the *No-Cry Solution* books.

Patti "The Wonderful" Hughes: my incredible, cheerful, and dependable assistant.

My husband, Robert: my partner, my friend, my love, my soul mate, and my sanctuary.

My family; my ultimate source of joy and inspiration: Mom, Vanessa, David, Coleton, Angela, Greg, Michelle, Loren, Sarah, Nicholas, Renée, Tom, Amber, Matthew, Devin, Tyler, and Wyatt.

All the readers who have written to me about their precious children. I feel a special friendship with each and every person who writes.

The many test mommies, daddies, and children for sharing a piece of their lives with me: Aaron, Abigael, Adelyn, Adriana, Agnes, Aiden, Ainslee, Alasia, Aleasha, Alex, Alexander, Alexandra, Alice, Alissa, Aliyah, Allison, Allyson, Alyssa, Amanda, Amara, Amber, Amelia, Amelie, Amy, Andr, Andrea, Andrew, Andy, Angel, Angelique, Ann, Anna, Anne, Anne-Cécile, Anneliese, Annie, Annika, Anoushka, Anusha, Archer, Aria, Ariana, Arwen, Asia, Aubrey, Audrey, August, Austin, Ayshwarya, Balin, Barbara, Barret, Becky, Bella, Ben, Benedict, Benjamin, Benji, Bobette, Brady, Brayden, Brendan, Brenna, Brennan, Brett, Bronwyn, Bryce, Cadence, Cai, Caitlyn, Caleb, Callie, Candice, Carolina, Carrie, Carson, Catherine, Catriona, Chace, Charlie,

Charlotte, Chase, Chris, Christian, Christine, Christoph, Cindy, Claire, Clare, Clea, Corrine, Cortney, Courtney, Cristina, Crystal, Cynthia, Daanyaal, Daisy, Dalton, Daniel, Dashiell, David, Dawn, Daza, Dazaï, Dean, Declan, Denise, Destiny, Diana, Dino, Donovan, Drew, Dylan, Edan, Effath, Eli, Elijah, Ellise, Emerson, Emilio, Emily, Emma, Erin, Erynne, Ethan, Evan, Evelynn, Faeryn, Fernando, Finnegan, Francelyne, Franziska, Gabriela, Gavin, Genevieve, Gianni, Giulio, Gloria, Grace, Graciela, Grayson, Hannah, Hayde, Hayden, Hazel, Heather, Hector, Henry, Hilary, Holly, Imogen, Isaac, Isabel, Isabelle, Jack, Jacob, Janet, Janie, Jarvis, Jason, Jekaterina, Jenifer, Jennifer, Jenny, Jensen, Jessica, Jill, Joanna, Joanne, Johnny, Jonah, Jonas, Jonathan, Joseph, Josh, Joshua, Joy, Jude, Judy, Jules, Julia, Julie, Justin, Kadence, Kael, Kaiya, Kate, Katherine, Kathleen, Katie, Kayleigh, Keaton, Kelly, Kenneth, Kertu, Kieran, Kimberly, Kirsten, Koda, Kristina, Laila, Laura, Lauren, Laurie, Layla, Leah, Leilah, Leonardo, Lesley, Letizia, Levi, Liam, Lily, Lilly, Lindi, Lisa, Loden, Lorenzo, Lorna, Louis, Lucas, Lucy, Luka, Luke, Lyla, Macy, Maddison, Madison, Maggie, Magnolia, Maia, Malcolm, Malissa, Mallorie, Marc, Maria, Marianne, Marie-Anne, Marina, Marlowe, Martha, Mary, Mary-Anne, Mason, Matteo, Matthew, Mattias, Maureen, Maxwell, Maya, Megan, Melanie, Melissa, Mia, Micah, Michael, Michelle, Miguel, Miles, Milo, Mina, Molly, Monica, Morgan, Nadine, Natalia, Nate, Nathan, Nathaniel, Neema, Neve, Nicholas, Nicole, Nikhil, Nikole, Noah, Noelia, Octavia, Oliver, Olivia, Owen, Paloma, Pamela, Pascual, Patti, Peyton, Pierce, Rachael, Rachel, Rebecca, Rebekah, Reed, Renée, Rianna, Rianne, Ricky, Ronan, Rosario, Rowan, Ryan, Saadia, Sabrina, Säde, Sage, Sam, Samantha, Sara, Sarah, Sarrah, Sean, Sebastian, Sebastien, Selene, Shannon, Sharee, Shawn, Sheshanna, Shriya, Siobhan, Sofía, Sol, Solene, Sophie, Soren, Stephanie, Steven, Stirling, Susan, Taegan, Tara, Teresa, Teri, Terra, Tessa, Theresa, Thomas,

Tiffany, Timothy, Tindi, Tobias, Toby, Tommy, Tracy, Tyler, Vanessa, Vasundhara, Victoria, Wes, Will, Yan, Yasmin, Yleana, Zaara, Zachary, Zane, Zanthias, Zaphira, Zara, Zarah, Zoey.

The Test Parents

During the creation of this book, I received input, ideas, questions, and glorious photos from an incredible group of test parents. These 172 people (parents to 294 precious children) let me peek into their families' picky eating problems and happy successes.

The No-Cry test parents live all over the world, and they represent all different kinds of families: married, single, unmarried partners, from one child up to five children, twins, triplets, adopted children, young parents, older parents, at-home moms, at-home dads, working parents, interracial families, multicultural families, and gay-parent families. The test mommies and daddies, as I affectionately call them, became my friends during this long and complicated process, and I believe I learned as much from them as they did from me. They are a varied and interesting group, as you can see:

Locations of the Test Families
- 85 from the United States: Alabama, Arizona, Arkansas, California, Colorado, Connecticut, Florida, Georgia, Idaho, Illinois, Indiana, Iowa, Kentucky, Louisiana, Massachusetts, Michigan, Minnesota, Mississippi, Missouri, Nebraska, New Jersey, New York, North Carolina, Ohio, Oklahoma, Pennsylvania, Tennessee, Texas, Utah, Vermont, Virginia, Washington, Wisconsin
- 24 from Canada: Alberta, British Columbia, Calgary, Ontario, Quebec

- 11 from Australia: New South Wales, Queensland, South Australia, Tasmania, Victoria, Western Australia
- 9 from the United Kingdom: England, Ireland, Scotland, Wales
- 8 from South Africa: Eastern Cape, Gauteng, Western Cape
- 5 from France: Centre, Lorraine, Massif Central
- 3 from New Zealand: Auckland, Gisborne, Rodney
- 3 from Spain: Barcelona, León, Madrid
- 3 from Ukraine: Kiev
- 3 from Germany: Ansbach, Vilseck
- 2 from Italy: Milan, Verona
- 2 from Cyprus: Limassol
- 2 from the Netherlands: Amsterdam, Assen
- 2 from Mexico: Coahuila, Querétaro
- 2 from Hong Kong: Discovery Bay
- 2 from Estonia: Harjumaa
- 2 from Bermuda: Southampton
- 1 from Kenya: Nairobi
- 1 from Indonesia: West Java
- 1 from Kuwait: Safat
- 1 from India: Mumbai

Children
- 138 girls
- 156 boys
- 5 sets of twins
- 38 babies (6 months to 12 months)
- 137 toddlers (12 months up to 3 years)
- 91 preschoolers (3 years to 6 years)
- 28 children (7 years to 9 years)

Introduction

189,800. That's the number of meals and snacks today's children can expect in their lifetime.* All that eating—not to mention preparing, serving, and cleaning—will take up a tremendous amount of their time. Eating should be a pleasurable experience. Food should not provoke anxiety, stress, or worry. Meals should supply the best possible fuel for energy, health, and emotional contentment. The act of eating—which will be done more often than almost anything else in your child's life—should be a positive, pleasant, enriching experience.

Most children leave their picky eating habits behind after a mere 3 to 5 percent of their entire lifetime of meals and snacks. So while your current struggles with your child's picky eating are real, important, and frustrating, they will pass in time. This long-term vision can enable you to view picky eating in a whole new light and reduce at least some of the pressure you may feel over the food situation in your house.

Looking at your child's life today, though, it's still important to work toward improving her diet, since children grow so rapidly during these early years, and they need appropriate nutrition for proper growth. In addition, you are setting some patterns that might remain with your child for a lifetime. According to Aristotle, "The habits we form from childhood make no small difference, but rather they make all the difference." The emotions that exist at your family dinner table, the memories attached to

---

* According to researchers half of all children born after 2007 in industrialized nations can expect to live to age 104 or older. Thus, 3 meals plus 2 snacks per day, 365 days per year for 104 years equals 189,800.

certain foods, the habits surrounding food choices, and the times and ways your family eats can all etch a permanent picture in your child's mind.

There will never be another time when you hold so much power to affect your child's future than right now. What this means is that his picky eating actions are only a symptom of childhood, and your response to these actions can become pivotal to his future.

Certainly, many of us who were picky eaters or who filled up on junk food, sugar, and soda day after day during childhood have grown to become careful, responsible eaters. However, it's likely that this has come about only after much effort, concentration, and self-discipline. How much easier it can be if healthy eating habits are instilled in childhood!

Every day should begin with a breakfast that is a pleasant, revitalizing start to the day. Snack time should be an energizing yet peaceful break between meals. Lunchtime is an opportunity for a midday connection and enjoyable refueling. The family dinner table should be a place of joy, relaxation, and bonding, as well as wholesome, healthy meals. In other words, the rituals that surround food and eating should be pleasant.

When you have a picky eater in the house, it can distort your vision of both the moment and the future. It can turn what should be happy moments into major battles. I polled my test parents and asked them how they felt about the food situation in their house. The most common word they used was *frustrated*; it was listed as the foremost emotion by 61 percent of respondents. Lest you feel your own emotions are unusual, scan the following words that were chosen by parents to describe their feelings about their child's picky eating habits:

- Overwhelmed
- Distressed

- Consumed
- Defeated
- Paralyzed
- Tortured
- Helpless
- Hopeless

As you can see from the list, dealing with a picky eater can be emotionally difficult for parents, and any of these feelings are normal. I believe it helps to know that your emotions are similar to other parents in your situation.

Keep Your Eye on the Goal

As the parent of a young child, you probably feel utterly responsible for his life and well-being. When your child refuses to do the most basic yet most necessary act of eating, it can be frightening. It can cause your protective instincts to move into overdrive—"I can't let my child starve!" I am here to tell you that your child will not starve; actually, he's not even at a slight risk of wasting away. He actually could survive on Goldfish crackers, cheese, and chicken nuggets until his picky eating stage ran its course. That would not be the best fuel for him, of course, but he'd still be running circles around most adults.

I encourage you to internalize the following concept: what is most important is *not* that your child ingest food, but rather that the food he does eat provides him with the vitamins, minerals, and sources of energy he needs to grow and thrive. A smaller amount of food than you would imagine can fit the bill—as long as it is the right kind of food. That will be our goal: to revise your child's current eating preferences into healthy habits that can sustain him with a minimum amount of fuss and stress.

> **Key Point**
> If your child is a picky eater, keep the correct goal in mind. The objective is not to make your child eat *more* food but to be sure that food choices are healthy ones.

What's Covered in *The No-Cry Picky Eater Solution?*

Part 1 provides a short but informative summary of picky eater facts: what's normal, what causes picky eating, and why it's so important to help your child become less finicky. Part 2 presents some essential concepts to get you started in making a plan to combat picky eating in your home. You'll also find handy charts to help you figure out the correct portions and serving sizes for your child's meals and snacks. Part 3 contains a multitude of tips, tricks, and tactics to handle every sort of food-related issue with a calm, organized plan of action. Part 4 gives you a terrific bonus—a collection of fantastic recipes designed for children's palates and provided by a group of well-respected and much-loved family cookbook authors.

The No-Cry Philosophy

This book, like all my *No-Cry Solution* books, is about finding respectful, effective solutions to your family's problems. It's about avoiding tears, stress, and anger and making positive changes in the most productive ways. The No-Cry philosophy is about viewing problems in the context of the complete child and the entire

Isaac, two years old

family. It is about solving only those issues that *you* feel are problems. Every family views food issues differently, and how you go about achieving your healthy eating goals will be different from how other families do it. Just because there is a section about how to help your toddler sit at the dinner table until the meal is over doesn't mean you have to force your child to sit. If you are happy with your child eating at his plastic picnic table and then going off to play the minute he's done eating, then go right ahead and let him—there's no harm in it. However, if you and your child are struggling in this area, and you'd like to help him become happy sitting at the table with you, then I will provide you with ideas for making this change that will help you stay calm and controlled and that will encourage your child to cooperate willingly.

So your first and foremost job is to decide what you want to change and why. As part of the process of change, consider why you feel any specific issue needs to be resolved. Is this truly something that must be addressed for your child's health and growth?

Is it of particular importance to you? Is it a battle that's worth fighting? For example, every child needs to eat vegetables to be healthy. *That* is the time to use every trick in the book. But many other food issues can be bypassed, either because they aren't that important, or because your child will naturally outgrow them.

When faced with a food issue, take the time to pull yourself out of the emotional fray for a moment and ask yourself these questions:

- Am I considering making changes because of input from outsiders, unnecessarily rigid rules, a power struggle with my child, or memories of my own childhood?
- Am I focused on the issue at hand, or am I being guided by worries about potential future problems that don't even exist right now?
- Is this issue something that truly affects my child's health— or our family peace—and so must be addressed now?

Mother-Speak

"My feeling is that people make a very big deal of eating when it should be something light and enjoyable. Children should be encouraged to have an open attitude to it, but for that, the parents need to lighten up."

—Sheshanna, mother of two-year-old Dazaï

There are no cookie-cutter solutions to any parenting problem, including picky eating. Therefore, I will provide an assortment of ideas for each situation. Pick one, pick two, or combine a variety of ideas to create a personalized plan for your child. Then adjust and modify your plan as you go until you find the right solution. That's how the process of raising children works best.

With this concept in mind, let's start with a crucial principle that I urge you to keep as a guiding light throughout the rest of this book—and, for that matter, the rest of your life. It can be applied to almost any parenting decision you'll face from now through grandchildren and even your *great*-grandchildren.

The No-Cry Process for Peaceful Problem Solving

There are no absolute rules about raising children and no guarantees for any parenting techniques. Raise your children as you choose, in ways that are right for you and protect their growth and development. Within the range of your comfort zone, modify your approach for each of your children based on their needs, personality, health, and temperament.

Address only those problems that you believe are true problems, and don't create or imagine problems because someone else thinks you have them—regardless of whether that person is family, friend, or expert.

Keep your problems in perspective, and take ample time to plot the best course of action. Solve your problems by analyzing possible solutions and choosing those that are right for you and your family. Know that there is rarely one right answer, and you must often take multiple routes to get to the best destination.

Read, listen, and learn constantly, but always sift what you learn through the strainer of your own personal beliefs and parenting philosophy.

Keep in mind both your short-term goals and your long-range goals. And remember to enjoy the days and moments along the way.

1

What You Really Need to Know About Picky Eaters

Parents face a number of common problems during their children's early years. Among them are sleep issues, potty training hurdles, temper tantrums, and—of course—picky eating. All these issues are rooted in normal childhood behavior, and all of them can create intense stress for parents. Picky eating can be one of the worst, because food is the fuel for growth and development, and you need to feed your child three meals plus snacks—*every single day*. This provides ample opportunity for ongoing frustration. You may feel like feeding issues overshadow every part of your life and put a damper on what should be an enjoyable stage in your child's growth.

When I polled my group of test parents about their picky eater situations, I found many common themes. No matter where in the world they live, no matter how many children in the household, and no matter what parenting style they follow, the details and emotions reveal similar themes. Parents everywhere reported these universal stories:

- "My child eats the same few foods every day, and they aren't healthy choices."
- "Vegetables are totally off-limits unless they are dripping in cheese sauce or dip."

- "New food is treated as foreign and suspicious, and my child refuses to try anything that isn't familiar."
- "I feel like I'm running a restaurant! I'm constantly making custom meals for my picky eater, and even then there's no guarantee she'll eat or even take a bite."
- "When I fix a plateful of healthy options, I feel like I throw most of it away. Either that, or I end up eating my portion and his too!"
- "Other people have said that my child is trying to control me with his food demands and that I should just 'be firm.' They have no idea how impossible that really is!"
- "People say my child is just being stubborn and willful and that I shouldn't let him get away with it, but I can't open his mouth and make him eat!"
- "I've been told that I'm responsible, that my actions have actually caused my child's picky eating habits. I know I haven't been perfect in this area, but it's not like I serve him cookies all day!"

Picky Eating Is Normal Behavior

Picky eating is a universal problem for parents during the early childhood years. It's popular to blame picky eating on weak, indulgent parents and stubborn, power-seeking kids. But after months of research and interviews with several hundred parents, I can confidently say that this theory is totally off the mark.

When surveyed, nearly 85 percent of parents say they have a child who is or has been picky about food. Almost half say they feel their child doesn't eat enough vegetables. And most parents feel their child doesn't eat a well-balanced diet. This tells us that a clear majority of families have at least one picky eater in the house. When I read that statistic, I knew there was no way that all those parents were indulgent and all those children willful every day, let alone at every meal. There must be more to this story.

Anytime I discover that a majority of children share a trait, that tells me it is normal childhood behavior, so I seek to find the reasons that it's so common. I'm always amazed at what I discover, and this time was no exception. I found many fascinating and compelling reasons why picky eating has nothing whatsoever to do with parenting style or stubbornness!

Even though a behavior is normal (and we'll get into that shortly), that doesn't mean we can't do something about it. Armed with the knowledge of where picky eating comes from and a variety of tips and solutions, we can help our picky eaters to get the proper daily nutrition they need and to expand their dietary options over time.

What Exactly Is a Picky Eater?

There isn't an exact scientific definition of "picky eater," but the term does encompass certain behaviors in regard to what a child will or won't eat and how he responds to food. While every parent defines the phenomenon a bit differently, the overall picture of a picky eater is pretty clear. It can help you to know that your child's behavior is similar to that of many other children and that your response is normal too.

In this book, we'll be talking about healthy, normal kids with typical eating habits. Your child can be classified as a typical picky eater if most—or all—of these statements are true:

- My child will eat only a small selection of foods.
- My child eats the same favorite foods almost daily.
- My child's diet consists of too much unhealthy food and too little nutritious food.
- My child complains about or refuses to eat the food I serve.

- My child does not eat the recommended three square meals plus two snacks each day.
- My child does not eat the recommended three to five servings of vegetables each day.
- My child prefers bread, noodles, and crackers made with refined white flour rather than those made with whole grains.
- My child's eating patterns change throughout the day, the week, and the month—sometimes he goes for long periods without eating, and other times he seems very hungry.

It's likely that you agreed with most or all of these statements, since the majority of picky eaters have similar habits. It's important, though, to make the distinction between typical picky eating habits and food issues that signify a physical or emotional problem. You can tell whether your child's picky eating habits are an immediate health concern or normal picky eater behavior by reading through these comments:

- My child has plenty of energy.
- My child is usually happy.
- My child's height and weight is within the normal range according to our health care provider.
- My child urinates four to nine times a day (every two to three hours or so) and has regular bowel movements that are soft and easy to pass at least once every day or two.
- My child has bright eyes, clear skin, healthy teeth, and good muscle tone.
- My child sleeps well, getting ten to twelve hours of sleep at night, plus naps when necessary.
- Over the course of a week, my child eats something from each of these food groups: grains; dairy; fruits; vegetables; proteins (including meat, fish, beans, soy, nuts, and seeds); and healthy fats and oils.

If you agreed with most or all of these statements, then we've identified your child as a typical picky eater. If this list does not describe your child, then there may be more going on than simply picky eating. I'd recommend that you take the list and your responses to your health care professional for discussion and problem solving.

Now, let's see how you fit into the picture, since parents respond in similar ways. You are a normal, loving parent of a typical picky eater if most or all of the following comments describe you:

- I worry that my child doesn't eat enough at many meals or on a given day.
- I'm concerned that my child doesn't eat enough vegetables, whole grains, and/or lean proteins.
- I believe that my child eats too much of the wrong foods—processed foods, refined white flour, and sugar.
- I have pleaded, begged, or bribed my child to eat.
- I have gotten upset or angry because my child won't eat or won't eat the right foods.
- I feel guilty because my child doesn't have a healthy diet.
- When my child doesn't eat or doesn't eat right, I feel that it's my fault.
- I don't know how to get my child to eat better, but I really want to achieve this goal.

It's quite possible that you've agreed with most or all of these statements, because they are the common feelings of parents of picky eaters. Once you realize how totally normal you are and how typical your child is, you can eliminate (or at least reduce!) the guilt and stress you feel over her eating habits. If you can calm your inner self and clear your head, then you can move forward toward creating a plan to help your child eat healthier.

Your Picky Eater Is Just Being a Kid

The biggest problem that parents of picky eaters face is the perpetuation of the myths that children should want to eat healthy, well-rounded meals every day, eat vegetables with gusto, never desire junk food, and emphatically turn down sweets and treats in favor of fresh fruit. Let's put these myths aside as wishful thinking and examine what real children are like:

- According to Abbott Nutrition in Singapore, picky eating is a worldwide problem. Some polls show that as many as 75 percent of parents say their child is, or has been, a picky eater. Adding those who say their child is "sometimes" picky raises that number to almost 85 percent.
- Up to 67 percent of parents say that vegetables are essentially "off-limits" to their little one.
- About 25 percent of parents report that their child refuses to try a new food when it's offered.
- A third of parents say their picky eater could survive on the same three to five foods every single day.
- Half of all picky eaters won't eat mixed dishes; they prefer individual foods that don't touch each other.
- The typical age span for picky eating is from fifteen months to six years, but it remains common up to about age ten and can persist in some children up to adolescence.
- A quarter of parents find their child's picky eating habits "beyond frustrating."

Is Picky Eating Dangerous?

Only a very small percentage of young children go beyond normal picky eating habits to the danger point where they lack the nutrients they need for healthy growth. These few children are truly stressed over food-related issues or have trouble with the physical mechanics of eating. They don't have normal growth and lack energy. If you have any concerns about your child's eating habits, it's always wise to talk to your health care provider.

Why Kids Are So Picky

Children are unique individuals, so each one's picky eating habits may have different causes. Regardless of the details surrounding your dinner table, your child's selective eating habits are likely to fall into one or more of the following general descriptions. It may be helpful to review these varied causes so you can better understand the background of picky eating and reduce any feelings of guilt, anger, or confusion you may have. This information can also help you set an effective plan for getting the picky eater in your family to improve and expand his diet.

It's About Genetic Connections

Science is still trying to sort this one out, but studies tell us that if one or both parents were picky eaters as children, chances are their child will be a picky eater too. Some studies show that if you disliked broccoli, fish, or fuzzy foods (such as peaches and kiwis) when you were a youngster, then chances are your child will dislike

---

Mother-Speak

"I was an extremely picky eater as a child and even as a young adult. My sister says that I ate by color—the only things I ate were beige: french fries, pasta, potatoes, crackers, bread, turkey, and chicken."

—Amy, mother of two-year-old Levi

the same sort of foods, since certain likes and dislikes may be part of her makeup. Researchers have found that genetic makeup also determines the number of sweet and sour taste buds a child is born with, determining which foods are naturally favored over others.

This genetic function tells us that while family habits and parents' response to food issues certainly have an effect on children's eating habits, inherited differences also come into play. Since each child has two parents, let's hope your child inherits the broccoli lover's genes, if you have those roaming around in your bloodline. If you have both been picky eaters in the past, it's no wonder you're reading this book today!

Professional-Speak

"While scientists once believed that all variation in food preference was learned, we now know that some of the variation is biological."

—**Cristian Boboila, Molecular, Cellular, and Developmental Biology and Economics, Yale College**

It's About Evolution and Instinct

Breast milk, baby's natural first food, has a sweet flavor. Fruits that are safe for humans to eat, such as strawberries and oranges, are also sweet. Poisonous plants, toxic chemicals, and spoiled foods, however, are sour or bitter, so a child's natural instinct is to avoid anything with those types of flavors. "If we just went running out of the cave as little cave babies and stuck anything in our mouths, that would have been potentially very dangerous," says Lucy Cooke, Ph.D., of University College, London.

Daisy, three years old

In today's world, this protective instinct is still important. It protects children from eating something that is rancid or poisonous. As soon as a child detects a sour or bitter flavor, his natural impulse is to spit the substance out—a good idea in many cases. Unfortunately, the compounds that provide vegetables with their health benefits are in the bitter range, so a child's aversion to vegetables may be based on his natural instinct.

Babies and toddlers put nearly anything in their mouths, but they (usually!) don't actually eat the plastic, metal, dirt, rocks, and other substances they orally explore; you could call this nature's safety gate. They'll mouth an object, lick it, chew it—and then spit it out. That's because their taste buds don't recognize the foreign flavor and tell them it's not something to eat. (Let them pick up a piece of a cookie or leftover candy bar, though, and down the hatch it goes.) This protective instinct is important but contributes to a child's narrow range of desired flavors.

These are important concepts to consider when introducing children to foods that are sour, bitter, or tart. When you realize you're going against natural instinct, it can help you understand that your child's reluctance to try unusual new foods isn't necessarily a gesture of willfulness. It can also open you up to the idea of using recipes that sweeten some foods when introducing them to your child for the first time, such as adding a touch of cheese to cauliflower, mixing raisins with broccoli, or dipping carrot pieces in yogurt. Roasting vegetables slowly caramelizes them and brings out the sweetness, so this can also do the trick.

It's About Biology

Taste buds communicate flavors to the brain. Babies are born with more taste buds than adults, and these tiny organs cover the tongue plus the sides and roof of the mouth. Babies have a more enhanced recognition of sweet tastes. Their ability to distinguish

Professional-Speak

"When we're really young, our taste buds are especially attuned to sweet flavors. If you're offered bananas and berries at an early age, that level of sweetness will satisfy. But if you're given concentrated sweets, a taste for those intense sweets will follow you for the rest of your life."

**—Amy Lanou, senior nutrition scientist,
Physicians Committee for Responsible Medicine**

and enjoy other flavors increases over time as they grow. By the end of the teenage years, they will have a decreased predilection for sweet flavors and an expanded appreciation of other tastes. This isn't to say that adults don't like sweets, but their instinctual pull toward these foods is less intense and is also affected by knowledge and the ability to make proper food choices.

A link has been found between the preference for sweet foods and the rate of bone growth. When children are in high-growth periods, their preference for sweet foods is elevated; as their rate of bone growth slows, so does their taste for sweets. This may be due to the high-energy properties of foods that contain sugars; fast-growing children are very active and have much higher energy needs than adults. Children may also have a genetic inclination to seek out energy-dense foods—which would draw them more strongly to fats, grains, and sugars over low-fat, low-calorie vegetables that would require a much bigger serving to achieve the same calorie benefit.

Professional-Speak

"Children are programmed to like sweet taste, because it fills a biological need by pushing them toward higher energy sources."

—Danielle Reed, Ph.D., geneticist,
Monell Chemical Senses Center

It's About Anatomy

While all babies and young children have enhanced taste buds, about one-quarter of them are born "supertasters." That's not a superpower; it's the scientific label for children who have an unusually high number of taste buds. This gives them a heightened sense of taste, which means sweets are sweeter and sour and bitter flavors are more intense than for other little ones. This makes foods like vegetables, olives, grapefruit, and soy products off-putting, since they contain antioxidants and other chemicals that taste unpleasantly bitter to supertasters. These children may avoid some sweet and fatty tastes also, due to the increased intensity of flavor, and therefore limit their diet choices immensely. The silver lining here is that later in life supertasters are less likely to drink alcohol, chew tobacco, or smoke due to the unpleasant oral sensations. So keep this benefit in mind the next time you become frustrated with your little supertaster.

You may be able to tell if your child is a supertaster by taking a look at the back portion of his tongue with a flashlight and a magnifying glass. If you see many more of the little bumps that house taste buds than normal, odds are you have a supertaster. (You may have to check out a few other tongues for perspective, but you'll probably find plenty of kids willing to engage in the experiment.) As children get older, their taste buds become less plentiful and less sensitive, so even supertasters can come to enjoy a greater range of flavors.

Professional-Speak

"The sense of taste is an important determinant of what children eat. We know that young children eat what they like. We also know that many children do not like bitter tastes, thereby interfering with vegetable consumption and potentially limiting the intake of important nutrients."

—Julie Mennella, Ph.D., developmental psychobiologist and researcher, Monell Chemical Senses Center

It's About the Power of Smell

While basic tastes are centered on the tongue, our sense of smell strongly influences our discernment of different flavors. As much as 70–80 percent of flavor is actually based on a food's scent. This is part of the reason that we lose our desire to eat when we have a bad cold.

Babies and young children have an enhanced sense of smell and a natural attraction to the sweet fragrance of breast milk. Babies are actually able to pick their mother out of a group based on her scent alone, something an adult is typically unable to do.

A child's sense of smell is even more heightened when she's hungry, so the scent of food is magnified, becoming an important determining factor for whether or not she finds a food desirable. This supersniffing ability helps explain children's preference for the pleasant odor of sweet foods (think chocolate chip cookies baking) and an avoidance of foods with sour or bitter odors (brussels sprouts, anyone?).

Scent also affects your little one's food choices because familiar odors are soothing to children, and they'll likely be drawn to food that carries a scent they recognize. Strange smells are cause for question, which is one more reason that children often avoid new and different foods.

It's About Food as a Total Experience

Children experience food differently than adults. In the same way that a child learns about toys, nature, or any object by touching, smelling, and manipulating things, he applies this same method of experimentation to food. A child is drawn to explore a food's shape, color, and texture. He wants to know the properties it displays—does it squash, flatten, pile up, or melt? If left to his own devices, he'll investigate how the food looks, smells, feels, and responds to his touch. The results of these investigations can help him decide if he'll take a taste. Even then, he'll further his exploration of how the food feels in his mouth. Is it crunchy? Smooth? Chewy? Does the flavor change as he eats it? Does it break apart or smooth together as he chews? If he doesn't like the end result, you can be sure he won't be shy about spitting it out! This entire process is part of the natural curiosity of childhood.

It's About the Pull of Familiarity

Many researchers believe that certain foods become familiar prenatally, since fetuses swallow and "breathe" the amniotic fluid that carries some of the flavors in the mother's diet. The foods that a mother eats repeatedly while pregnant can influence the future food preferences of her baby. For example, a study at the Monell Chemical Senses Center in Philadelphia, Pennsylvania, showed that mothers who drank carrot juice daily while pregnant had babies who enjoyed the taste of carrots much more than those whose mothers did not drink the juice.

Breast-feeding babies will also detect flavors through their mother's breast milk. All babies will be exposed to the aroma of the family's typical foods for a long time before tasting them.

Children are reassured by rituals, routines, and familiarity in their lives, so cultural habits can affect what foods they eat. When it comes to diet, they are influenced by the food they are exposed to every day. To understand this, you only need to look at the "traditional" breakfast foods in different cultures: American children will tend toward cereal, toast, eggs, and pancakes; children in India will have curry-flavored foods; children in Guatemala will likely eat beans and corn tortillas; and Japanese children will experience a typical breakfast of rice, soup made with soy, and fish. Since it takes repeated exposure to a flavor for a child to accept it, the foods that frequent your family's table will become your child's staples as well.

Matteo, one year old

Keep in mind that intensity of flavor is an acquired taste. An interesting point that demonstrates the universal acceptance of children's dietary sensitivity is that, in nearly every culture, parents provide a milder version of everyday cuisine for little ones, allowing them to become accustomed to the spices and flavors before introducing them to the full-intensity adult version. By that point, the child has become used to the smell, texture, and general flavor and is likely to welcome the more potent recipe.

Most children search for order in their lives. They love predictable routines and consistent events. They'll sing the same song over and over; they'll ask you to read their favorite book to them over and over; and they'll play with their favorite toys every single day. Children who are picky eaters often have a limited menu of foods they will eat, and through force of habit, they will gravitate toward these familiar and comforting foods.

Many picky eaters incorporate food into their daily routine and don't like to veer from that path. For example, if your child always has chocolate milk, cheese, and Goldfish crackers when she gets up from her nap, she *always* wants chocolate milk, cheese, and Goldfish crackers when she gets up from her nap. If you try to give her white milk, yogurt, and whole-grain crackers, she'll feel out of sorts and off-kilter, and you'll likely have a food battle on your hands.

It's About Growth

Babies grow fast—most triple their birth weight during the first year of life. That amazing growth is fueled by a constant need for food. Breast-fed babies can nurse from ten to fifteen (or even more) times a day, and formula-fed babies up to ten or more times a day. As babies turn into toddlers, their rate of growth slows down, so they need to eat less food and eat less frequently. Parents who are used to feeding a baby every few hours need to adjust to a new reduced-food schedule.

After that first year of rapid growth, children will have a more gradual growth curve, spikes of growth spurts followed by periods of slower growth, and their appetites will reflect this up-and-down pattern.

Toddlers are very active and more interested in moving and exploring than eating. However, they do have an appetite control center in their brain that helps regulate when and how much they eat. They will often eat in spurts, filling up with food at one meal and skimping on the next.

Children will experience this burst-and-pause process of development throughout their growing years, which will affect how much they eat at any given stage.

It's About Control

Children have little control over what goes on in their lives. Someone is always telling them what to do, when to do it, and how to do it. They must do many things they don't want to do, such as go to day care, attend school, leave the park, or go to bed. One of the few things over which a child has ultimate control is the food that goes in his mouth and down his throat. This is one of the times that he actually has the final say: no matter how hard anyone tries, they cannot *make* a child swallow something!

While control may be a factor in picky eating and can affect a certain number of interactions, it is unlikely to be the primary factor. No child has the ability or consistency to fight with every adult over every meal and snack. However, a child who hates the taste of cabbage may find that food worth fighting over every time it's put on his plate. A child who eats an excess of junk food and sweets will become hooked on them and be willing to nag, whine, and beg until she gets what she wants.

It's About a Lack of Wisdom

As an adult, it's likely that many of the foods you eat each day are not necessarily chosen because they are tasty but because you know they are healthy for you. It's possible that you choose to eat salmon, rice, and green beans for dinner instead of an ice cream sundae because you know it's the healthier choice. I would love to eat a big chocolate chip muffin for breakfast, but I don't do it because I know it would be a huge serving of empty calories. I don't care for blueberries, but I put them in my oatmeal every morning because I know they provide a great burst of vitamins, minerals, antioxidants, and fiber to start my day.

Young children don't share our wisdom of diet and nutritional value. Add that to all of the aforementioned reasons for picky eating, and it makes perfect sense that most children would choose the sweet, delicious ice cream sundae or chocolate chip muffin whenever possible. This youthful disregard is just one more factor in typical picky eating behavior.

The Power of Early Experiences

Once you review the many reasons that children are picky eaters you'll see what a parent is really up against! As you try to feed your child a balanced, healthy diet, it can be quite a challenge to battle all that nature throws in front of you. Many parents, coming up against a wall of resistance over and over again, simply give up and feed their child whatever it is he will eat. The problem with this approach is that it becomes a vicious cycle. Your child won't eat healthy food; you feed him the nutrient-poor substitutes; he becomes accustomed to these foods; he won't eat the healthy food you offer. By the time your child outgrows these dietary limitations, his food habits are set in place and harder to change.

Research shows that food preferences are established early in life. One study by the University of Tennessee followed seventy mother-baby pairs for eight years. Researchers discovered that the foods the children liked at age two or three were usually the same foods they were eating at age ten. This gives parents a tremendous amount of power and responsibility to shape their children's future in previously unrecognized ways. It speaks loudly to the fact that we should use great care in choosing the types of foods we feed our children from a young age.

Professional-Speak

"In most cases, parents, particularly mothers, are the gate-keepers of what babies eat. Mothers tend not to offer their babies food they dislike themselves. So if Mom can't bear brussels sprouts, chances are her child will never taste them."

—**"Rethinking First Foods,"** *Time*, June 11, 2006

The Importance of Knowing Food Facts

Would you put motor oil instead of soap in your dishwater? Would you water your lawn with paint thinner? Would you put muddy water in your car's gas tank? Would you feed an energetic, growing child a diet filled with refined sugars, highly processed food products, and preservatives but lacking in nutritional value? While the answers to these questions are ridiculously obvious, a vast number of children are totally missing the mark on the healthy diet that would enable them to achieve their maximum health and fitness. Providing your child with good nutrition every single day can be a complicated mission, and many well-intentioned parents don't understand some important facets to their child's daily diet.

You may have a child who refuses to taste anything new, who seems to get by on a handful of crackers and half a banana, or who is more interested in building with blocks than eating lunch. No matter what your picky eater challenges are, it's important that you know a few of the critical facts about children and nutrition as you embark on a plan to change the routines in your home. This will help you make the right choices and pick the right battles. In addition, most parents find it helpful to learn that their challenges are not unique—on the contrary, the picky eating issues you struggle with in your own home are likely the same as those faced by the majority of families the world over. For all these reasons, I'd like to share a few facts and statistics with you, after which we'll move on to Parts 2 and 3 for tips and practical solutions for expanding your picky eater's culinary horizons.

The Fact: Food Affects Mood

A well-balanced diet can improve a child's mood and prevent the tantrums, fussing, and whining that accompany the mood swings brought about by hunger and lack of nutrients. In a nutshell, the scientific connection between food and mood is this: the substances we ingest bring about changes in our brain function, which directly affects our behavior. One study of adults conducted in Great Britain by the Food and Mood Project found that 80 percent of people with mood disorders were able to connect their moods directly with the foods they ate. There is no doubt that a mind-body connection exists.

Children who have food sensitivities or allergies can suffer mood swings, unexplained anger, fatigue, and hyperactivity after eating offending foods. When allergies go undetected, a child may be eating the wrong things at almost every meal, making it difficult to identify which foods are actually responsible for these symptoms.

In addition to the actual chemical changes food causes in the body, children's blood sugar levels naturally fluctuate during the course of the day, and the time lag between eating—as well as the types of foods they eat—directly affect this fluctuation. When children eat a diet high in sugar, refined carbohydrates, and junk food that's low in protein and fiber, it's a challenge for their system. On top of that, many kids go for long periods of time without eating, creating added stress to their body. Blood sugar fluctuations become extreme and numerous, leading to emotional meltdown, stubbornness, tantrums, whining, and fussing.

In contrast, a healthy, balanced diet eaten in regularly spaced meals and snacks has a pleasant and powerful effect on a child's mood, stabilizing his emotions and resulting behavior.

The Shocker

A survey completed by the American Dietetic Association Foundation found that many children miss regular meals. The research found that more than 40 percent of children do not always eat breakfast, and an estimated 22–38 percent completely skip dinner.

It may surprise you to learn that, in addition to experiencing associated mood swings, those children who skip meals are significantly *heavier* than those who eat three meals a day, and meal-skippers are at a higher risk for lifetime obesity. The main reason for this is that missed meals often lead to cravings for high-fat snacks throughout the day and an inability to monitor serving sizes, resulting in excess calories without the good nutritional value that would have been found in a balanced meal.

Even those children who *do* eat often enough are consuming a disproportionately large amount of refined carbohydrates and sugar instead of healthy whole grains, vegetables, fruits, and protein. A majority of children today get more than a quarter of their daily calories from junk food—nutritionally weak foods that are high in refined carbohydrates and sugar. Children are tempted by unhealthy food choices every day, and they don't have the knowledge, self-discipline, or foresight to make the right choices for themselves.

The Solution

Set a daily meal schedule for your child that includes breakfast, lunch, dinner, and two or three small snacks between meals. Teach your child to listen to his body cues, have something healthy to eat when he's hungry, and avoid junk food as a quick fix to hunger. For a guideline on the proper portions and serving sizes for meals and snacks, review the food charts in Part 2.

Laila, three years old

The Fact: Excess Sugar Affects Your Child's Health

Research shows that babies are born with an innate preference for sweet tastes, and this preference remains strong throughout childhood. I'm sure a scientist didn't have to tell you that—you've probably figured it out yourself!

It's hard to steer children away from sugar, since sweet foods abound. They surround your child in stores, at friends' homes, at grandparents' houses, on television, and probably in your own kitchen. Sweets are irresistibly attractive, and their pleasing flavor makes them enticing. In addition to the obvious sweet treats, sugar lurks in the everyday foods that fill your cabinets, such as cereal, yogurt, bread, soups, condiments, peanut butter, crackers, canned fruit, pancake mix, and many other items.

While a bit of sweetness is enjoyable for any child, excess sugar in a child's diet can lead to tooth decay and obesity, as well as the many problems that being overweight brings, such as hypertension, heart disease, and diabetes. Too many sweet treats can also result in vitamin deficiencies—a shortage of calcium and other vitamins and minerals—because sugary snacks and drinks fill your child with empty calories and take the place of more healthy foods and beverages. Other potential dangers include a suppressed autoimmune system and an increased risk of asthma, migraines, depression, emphysema, eczema, arthritis, gallstones, and heart disease.

Cookies, candy, ice cream, and other sweets are culprits, of course, but children also get a supersized serving of sugar from soda and processed juice drinks, which add more sugar to a typical preschooler's diet than all those other goodies combined. (See pages 38–39 for more information about the problems with soda.)

Sugar is absorbed into a child's system very quickly and causes a rapid peak in blood sugar, but it then falls dramatically after an hour or two. This up and down in blood sugar level can cause moodiness and emotional meltdowns. Some studies show that a certain percentage of children are sugar-sensitive, which enhances the negative effects of sweets. Kathleen DesMaison, Ph.D., author of *Little Sugar Addicts*, explains that the biochemical condition of sugar sensitivity that some children suffer brings on mood swings, erratic behavior, loss of concentration, fatigue, and crankiness. She believes that reducing the amount of sugar in these children's diets is the simple yet powerful solution to reducing these effects.

The Shocker

According to information recorded by the American Dietetic Association, the typical child gets more than 20 percent of her daily calories from sugar, some in candy and soda and some hidden in everyday foods. In real terms, that means children consume up to twenty-nine teaspoons of sugar *per day*. More than 60 percent of toddlers gulp down desserts, sweets, and sweetened beverages on a regular basis, and some studies show that by the time they are two years old, one in five children are eating candy every day! I wouldn't be surprised if the number of school-age kids eating sugary treats every day has inched up toward 100 percent.

Mother-Speak

"I signed on to a website food-tracker for myself that counts calories, fat, protein, fiber, and sugar. Yesterday I decided to log in my daughter's food for the day. I nearly fell over when I saw that she ate *twice* the recommended amount of sugar! I had no idea that sugar was lurking in so much of her food."

—**Nicole, mother of four-year-old Victoria**

Does 12 pounds of sugar per year sound like a lot? That's what the average adult consumed—in the 1880s. Today, that amount has jumped to *more than 150 pounds* of sugar per person, per year. The reason for this remarkably high quantity is that sugar is not just found in candy, cookies, and soda; it's an ingredient in a majority of packaged foods and beverages, listed under a variety of different names (see the following list). Many supposedly healthy food products like energy bars, juice drinks, fruit snacks, and yogurt contain sugar as a key ingredient.

In addition to added sugars, you'll find natural sugar in many foods such as fruit, milk, and yogurt. Some children are lactose intolerant, which can make the natural sugars in dairy products difficult to digest and cause cramps, gas, nausea, and diarrhea, plus the fussiness that goes along with the discomfort.

Natural sugars, as well as a controlled sprinkling of sweets, can be part of a healthy diet, but the common excess pounds of added sugars are not good for anyone—let alone an energetic, growing child!

Foods that contain sugar don't necessarily cite the word *sugar* on their list of ingredients. The following substances are different forms of sugar:

Barley malt	Galactose	Panocha
Beet sugar	Glucose	Polydextrose
Brown rice syrup	Glucose-fructose syrup	Powdered sugar
Brown sugar	High-fructose	Raw sugar
Cane juice	corn syrup*	Rice syrup
Confectioners'	Honey	Sorbitol
sugar	Lactose	Sucrose
Corn syrup	Maltitol	Sugar cane
Demerara	Maltodextrin	Treacle
Dextrose	Maltose	Turbinado sugar
Evaporated cane	Maple sugar	Xylitol
juice	Maple syrup	
Fructose	Molasses	

* High-fructose corn syrup is one of the most common ingredients found in a wide variety of processed foods and drinks. Research on this sweetener is ongoing and evolving, and it is a heated topic of discussion among dietary experts, so keep an eye out for news on this topic. Nonetheless, since sugars of all kinds are best used in moderation, and corn syrup is a processed form of sugar, it's best to avoid products that contain it whenever possible.

Replacing sugar with artificial sweeteners is not the solution. Imitation sweeteners continue to provide your child with a sweet taste, sometimes even sweeter than natural sugar. This really isn't the goal, as it will just reinforce your child's need for sweetness. In addition to providing an extreme flavor boost, artificial sweeteners do not add any nutritional value. Some chemical sweeteners carry health risks even more dangerous than excess sugar, such as headaches, depression, anxiety, dizziness, gastrointestinal distress, and possibly even cancer. Following is a list of artificial sweeteners:

Acesulfame potassium	Erythritol	Sorbitol
Alitame	Maltitol	Sucralose
Aspartame	Neotame	
Cyclamates	Saccharin	

Do your research on the sweeteners that are in your foods, but keep in mind that no definitive long-term studies have been completed to help you determine whether these additives are something you want to include in your child's diet, or yours. Thus, it's wise to avoid them as much as possible.

The Solution

Determine how much sugar is appropriate for your child and monitor her sugar intake on a daily basis. Read ingredient labels on packages to learn how many grams of sugar are in foods, and teach your child how to do this as well. Set specific rules about sweet treats so this doesn't become an ongoing battle between you and your child.

The Fact: Whole Grains Build Strong Bodies

Grains are an essential part of a healthy diet, but there is a world of difference between refined white (enriched) flour products and whole grains. Enriched flour really *isn't*, since many of the important nutrients are eliminated in the grinding and processing of refined flour, leaving only a fraction of the healthiest parts of the grains. The "enriching" is actually the addition of vitamins and minerals that are added back into the flour after the milling process is complete.

A whole grain kernel has three layers: the bran, the germ, and the endosperm. Each layer has important health benefits. The bran contains healthy fiber, the germ contains the majority of nutrients and healthy fats, and the endosperm is the starchy middle layer. Guess what refined white flour contains? Mostly the starchy, nutrient-stripped middle layer.

Brown rice is a whole grain, whereas white rice is much like refined flour in that the healthiest layers are removed. This strips the rice of nutrients and leaves mostly the starchy, less nutritious endosperm. In enriched white rice, like enriched flour, some of the missing nutrients are added back in.

Refined white flour and white rice are digested much like sugar is, causing a spike in blood sugar followed by a plunge. So when your child eats white-flour bread, rolls, crackers, or pasta or white rice, he's eating the least nutritious part of the grain; he's getting a spike and crash in energy level and missing out on the most important nutritional values of whole grains.

Whole grains are an important source of fiber, which is essential for proper digestion and elimination and helps to lower cholesterol and prevent diabetes. A diet rich in fiber can reduce the risk of heart disease and is one more key to preventing lifelong obesity. Fiber is critical to the prevention of constipation. It is a factor in cleansing the colon and preventing gas, bloating, and indigestion. You can boost fiber intake substantially by switching to whole-grain products over refined varieties.

In summary, when your child eats whole grains daily, he gains valuable benefits—vitamins, minerals, and fiber—that help him grow and potentially shield him from heart disease, diabetes, cancer, and obesity.

The Shocker

Nearly 100 percent of children eat plenty of grain products, but the average child eats *less than 20 percent* of those foods as healthy whole grains. Nine out of ten children do not get enough fiber in their diet.

The Solution

Whenever possible, choose whole grains over refined products for your child and yourself. If your little one is already accustomed to a diet of refined grains, use some of the solutions in the section "Top Ten Tips, Tricks, and Tactics" in Part 3 to gradually transition your child to healthier whole grains.

The Fact: Vegetables and Fruits Are Miracle Foods

The recommendation for eating plenty of vegetables and fruits every day is based on the fact that they provide an amazing amount of vitamins and minerals in the form of complex carbohydrates. They are slow to digest and remain in your child's system from meal to meal, preventing blood sugar highs and lows. Fruits and vegetables are nature's best source of dietary fiber, which is absolutely necessary for your child's digestive tract to work properly. As discussed earlier, getting ample fiber is one of the keys to preventing heart disease, diabetes, and cancer. These miracle foods also help prevent strokes and osteoporosis. A fiber-rich diet keeps weight under control and prevents constipation, which helps a child feel more energetic and makes potty training easier too.

A lifetime of including fruits and vegetables as part of their daily diet starts with habits that your children are forming now. New studies, including one by the American Heart Association, are showing that when children eat more vegetables early in life, they continue to eat these foods and, as a result, have healthier hearts, blood, and arteries as adults.

Tobias, four years old

The Shocker

More than 65 percent of parents report ongoing problems con-vincing their children to eat vegetables. The Feeding Infants and Toddlers (FITS) group studied children's eating habits and discov-ered some shocking news: almost a third of young children don't eat *a single serving* of vegetables on a given day, and more than 80 percent of kids do not eat dark leafy greens or orange vegetables routinely. FITS also found that a quarter of toddlers don't eat any fruit most days.

The Solution

Make it your personal mission to get your child to enjoy vegetables and eat them every day. To achieve this, you'll need to become a fan of vegetables yourself and learn new ways to prepare and serve them so that they become more enjoyable for everyone in the family. You'll find some great vegetable recipes in Part 4. You can also review the suggestions in Part 3, in the section "Put Vegetables on a Pedestal," to help your child achieve a lifetime of good health.

The Fact: Consuming Excess Sodium Is Unhealthy

You need a small amount of sodium to function properly, as it helps maintain a proper fluid balance in your body and aids muscle activity. Excess sodium, however, is unhealthy, and a surplus of sodium can be dangerous, leading to kidney problems or high blood pressure, which may result in heart disease or stroke. Excess sodium intake has also been linked to obesity, certain cancers, osteoporosis, and asthma.

Most processed food contains surplus salt, which is used to maintain product freshness in addition to enhancing flavor. Restaurant foods and packaged foods contain far more salt than most of us use in the kitchen. As a matter of fact, according to the Centers for Disease Control and Prevention (CDC), about 77 percent of the sodium we eat comes from packaged foods and restaurant meals.

The Shocker

The Institute of Medicine (IOM) recommends a daily intake of 1,000 milligrams of sodium for children aged one to three years and 1,200 milligrams for children aged four to eight years. However, the IOM has discovered that 76 percent of toddlers and 90 percent of preschoolers consume more than these healthy limits.

The Solution

People acquire a taste for salty foods. The more salt a child consumes, the more she will gravitate toward salty flavors, so if you minimize salt use from the start, your child won't miss it. A child who is currently consuming too much salt will easily adapt to a lower-salt diet if the amount is reduced over time. A small amount is all you need for flavor, so when cooking at home, reduce your use of salt or salted spices and rely on herbs or unsalted spices.

When shopping, look for low-sodium versions of processed foods or those without added salt. Choose fresh foods over processed whenever possible.

When eating at a restaurant, ask if meals can be prepared with less salt, and don't add extra salt at the table. Ask for sauces and dressings on the side, and use them sparingly. Request unsalted french fries if you order them for your children, as most fast-food restaurants are willing to accommodate this request. Many restaurant chains have online nutrition guidelines for menu items; scanning this information before ordering can help you make wise choices.

The Fact: Saturated Fats and Trans Fats Can Be Dangerous

Different categories of fats are found in food. Some are required for optimum health, but others are the total opposite—they prevent good health. Since all fats are not created equal, it's important to know the difference.

The body uses certain kinds of fats for energy. Your child is constantly on the move, so she needs an adequate amount of *unsaturated fats*. These are the healthy type of fats that contain essential fatty acids (EFAs), such as those found in fish, nuts, seeds, olives, avocado, soy, and olive oil. Essential fatty acids are especially important for a growing child; they play an important role in brain and eye development, and they help build cells, strengthen immunity, control the nervous system, and fortify the cardiovascular system.

Saturated fats (naturally occurring, animal-based fats, such as red meat, butter, whole milk, and full-fat ice cream) and *trans fats* (also called hydrogenated fats), which are created during food processing, are both considered the "bad" fats. While naturally occurring saturated fats are less of a danger than artificially created trans fats, eating a diet filled with either of them can lead to high cholesterol, clogged arteries, heart disease, and stroke. Hydrogenated fats can damage cellular membranes, such as those in the brain and nervous system—a critical concern for growing children. Trans and saturated fats interfere with the body's ability to metabolize the healthy fats that are so important to health and development.

The Shocker
According to the Office of Disease Prevention and Health Promotion, the daily fat intake for children over age two should total no more than 30–35 percent of their calories, with most fats being unsaturated. However, nearly 75 percent of children consume too much saturated fat, and more than a third do not get enough of the necessary healthy unsaturated fats in their daily diet. With the shocking increase in childhood obesity, the popularity of fast-food restaurants, and the real possibility of diabetes and other health problems cropping up even before adolescence, it's critical that we gain control of the amount and types of fat our children consume.

The Solution
The first step to reducing the amount of saturated and trans fats and increasing healthy unsaturated fats in your child's diet is knowledge, so become diligent about reading package labels and learning the fat content in your family's typical foods. Limit your use of butter, whole-fat dairy products, processed foods, and high-

fat red meat in favor of vegetable oils, low-fat dairy, fish, poultry, lean meat, and fresh whole foods.

The Fact: Chemicals, Hormones, Antibiotics, and Pesticides Are Present in Many Commercially Sold Foods

Growth hormones in beef, antibiotics given to food animals, pesticides on produce, and chemical additives in packaged foods— artificially altered foods crowd the supermarket. According to the World Health Organization, the contamination of food by chemical hazards is a worldwide public health concern. This contamination can come about through the air, water, and soil pollution or through the intentional use of chemicals during food growing, processing, and packaging. Studies show that certain levels of these additives can damage brain cells, increase the risk of cancer, and contribute to early puberty in children. Because of the dangers associated with such additives, many governmental agencies monitor the chemicals in our foods to be sure they don't reach hazardous levels.

The Shocker
Many of the tests done to determine the safety of chemicals used in foods apply specifically to adults. Whether these standards also apply to babies and children is not always clear. What is clear is that after children eat foods with these substances, residual amounts show up in their blood and urine tests. Furthermore, there have as yet been no tests done to determine the long-term effects of these additives; those studies that have been done are limited in scope, since these chemicals are toxic and cannot be tested directly on human beings.

Magnolia, two years old

The Solution

You can minimize your family's risk of food-borne illness and disease stemming from additives by being wise when shopping for and preparing food. Examine the foods you buy and read the labels. Properly clean, refrigerate, freeze, and cook food as recommended on the package. Wash all fresh produce thoroughly. When possible, purchase hormone-free meat and dairy products and organic produce. Plant your own garden or participate in a neighborhood gardening plot. Do your homework; learn about the issue and advocate for healthier food in your grocery stores and restaurants.

The Fact: Overweight Children Frequently Grow Up to Become Overweight Adults

Being overweight increases the risk for a wide variety of health issues, including heart disease, diabetes, stroke, arthritis, high blood pressure, liver disease, and some types of cancer. We're not talking about babies who are chubby from frequent breast-feeding, but of children who are carrying too much weight because of unhealthy eating habits.

Childhood obesity is not to be taken lightly, as it is a serious medical condition that can easily lead to dangerous health problems. It can also be a factor in a child's low self-esteem, which can lead to depression, socialization issues, and problems in school.

Professional-Speak

"Not all children carrying extra pounds are overweight or obese. Some children have larger-than-average body frames. And children normally carry different amounts of body fat at the various stages of development. So you might not know just by looking at your child if his or her weight is a health concern. Your child's doctor (or a nutritionist) can help you figure out if your child's weight could pose health problems. To do this, the professional will calculate your child's body mass index (BMI). The BMI indicates if your child is overweight for his or her age and height."

**—Mayo Foundation for Medical Education
and Research (MFMER), Mayo Clinic**

The Shocker

According to the World Health Organization, nearly 43 million children under the age of five were overweight in 2010; 20–40 percent of all children are overweight or obese; and another 25 percent are at risk of becoming overweight or obese if they continue their current eating habits. These percentages vary depending on location, but childhood obesity is a worldwide problem. The

National Health and Nutrition Surveys completed by the U.S. Department of Health and Human Services tell us that obesity among children has *more than tripled* since 1980 and quadrupled since 1970—and the numbers continue to rise. They warn that today's children may be "the first generation to live shorter, less healthy lives than their parents."

Professional-Speak

"I'm seeing younger and younger kids overweight—as young as ten months old. Parents bring babies into the office in these huge strollers packed with food and snacks, drinking soda and juice. We never used to see that."

—Jan Hangen, clinical nutrition specialist,
Children's Hospital Boston

The Solution

Children learn what they live, and this is especially true when it comes to eating habits. That's why it's important to teach them to eat mindfully. Teach your child how to make good food choices by discussing the properties and value of certain foods and food groups. Don't make this a painful, one-time lecture; rather, inject short conversations into everyday life. Discuss *why* she can't have a cookie for lunch and should have the healthy plate you've prepared instead. Don't use food as a reward or punishment, and avoid having family battles over food issues. Make family mealtime an enjoyable experience. Stock your refrigerator and pantry with healthy choices, limit junk food, and serve a well-balanced diet—making sure you eat one yourself—as your actions speak louder than your words.

The Fact: Eating Meals as a Family Is Good for Your Children's Health

Studies tell us that if you eat dinner together regularly as a family, your children will reap amazing benefits. Kids who eat meals with their parents acquire healthier food habits; are less likely to abuse alcohol, tobacco, and illegal drugs; become better students; are less likely to suffer from depression; and stay emotionally closer to their family. You and your children will benefit in other ways too. Numerous studies, including those conducted by the University of Minnesota and Harvard University, show that when a family has a routine of eating dinner together, everyone eats more vegetables, fruits, lean proteins, and whole grains.

The Shocker

In nearly half of all households, dinner is a family affair only a few days a week. Ten percent of families never eat dinner together at all. Only a quarter of families report eating dinner together most nights.

Although many families don't routinely eat together, kids really want them to! One fascinating 2010 study completed by the National Center on Addiction and Substance Abuse at Columbia University showed that 72 percent of teenagers felt that eating frequent family dinners together was important.

The Solution

Have dinner as a family as often as you can, because every meal you share counts. Don't be discouraged if you can't arrange this every day; just find another way to make a daily connection. If busy schedules prevent dinner with the entire group, then gather as many family members as possible or aim for a family breakfast or lunch. If a daily family meal isn't possible, you might even set up a prebedtime chat to create this camaraderie among family members.

Barret, six years old; August, one year old; and Oliver,
four years old

The Fact: Drinking Soda
Is Dangerous to Your Child's Health

Public health officials call soda "liquid candy." It's easy to see why:
there is no nutritional value in it, and a twelve-ounce can contains
nine to twelve teaspoons of sugar (a twenty-ounce bottle contains
sixteen to eighteen teaspoons). If you want a powerful mental picture of this, put eighteen teaspoons of sugar in a bowl—that's the
amount in one big bottle of soda pop!

The first problem with soda is obviously the addition of too
much sugar to your child's diet. The second problem is that it
replaces other more nutritious drinks, preventing your child from
getting important nutrients he needs for growth and development,
while adding to weight gain from empty calories and sugar.

Drinking soda daily can deplete calcium in the bones, leading to a bigger risk of broken bones and osteoporosis later in life. Regular soda drinking can increase the risk of diabetes and kidney problems. Soda also contains acid that weakens and erodes tooth enamel and contributes to tooth decay.

The Shocker

Twenty percent of toddlers drink an average of a cup of soda per day. That's the frightening statistic brought to light by the Center for Science in the Public Interest. Researchers also found that 56 percent of eight-year-old children drink soda daily, and that this number rises steadily with age. By the teen years, 83 percent of kids are soda drinkers, and they get 11 percent of their daily calories from these unhealthy nonnutritive beverages. One third of teenage boys drink three or more cans of soda per day—that adds up to 189 to 252 teaspoons of sugar per week. Many teens drink caffeinated sodas, which add caffeine dependence to the sugar habit. According to the U.S. Department of Agriculture, the consumption of soft drinks has increased 500 percent in the last fifty years.

The Solution

The solution is easy in theory but takes a strong parent to uphold: limit sodas to an occasional special event, such as a holiday party. Don't keep soft drinks in your home, since out of sight is out of mind. Serve water, milk, vegetable juice, and small amounts of fruit juice to your child as everyday beverages.

The Fact: Breakfast Really Is the Most Important Meal of the Day

By breakfast time, a child may have gone twelve to eighteen hours without food. Putting off nutrition even longer can be detrimental to her fast-growing brain and body. Compared to children who skip the first meal of the day, those who eat breakfast consume more vitamins, minerals, and fiber in their diets overall. They have more energy, fewer behavioral problems, less fatigue, and better memory. They also get better grades, miss fewer days of school, are less likely to have to repeat a grade, are more likely to maintain a healthy body weight and make better food choices for the rest of the day, and are generally in better health.

The Shocker

Dozens of studies from all over the world show that as many as 15 percent of young children regularly skip breakfast, and over 40 percent of youngsters report they occasionally pass on breakfast. By the teen years, as many as one-third of young people routinely miss this important meal. While the numbers vary depending on location and demographic and socioeconomic status, it's bad news for one child to miss breakfast, let alone these large groups.

The Solution

Make breakfast a ritual in your house. Aim for a healthy meal that contains at least two or three of the main food groups, but keep in mind that any breakfast is better than none. Many ideas are scattered throughout Part 3 to help you get your picky eater to enjoy a daily breakfast, including specific tips in the "Get a Sleepyhead to Eat a Good Breakfast" section.

Luke, two years old

The Fact: Young Children Learn Eating Habits Mainly from Their Parents

A portion of what a child learns about food, eating, and nutrition is accomplished through his ongoing discussions with his parents over time. Children will learn some information from teachers at school, but it's typically a very small amount, and it's offset by the poor examples provided by classmates and the unhealthy food offered in the school cafeteria or vending machines.

The largest percentage of a child's lessons about nutrition and food choice is likely achieved by the example set by the adults in his life. Children are remarkably perceptive, and they see and absorb far more than we think they do.

"Do as I say, not as I do" doesn't work when creating eating habits. If parents are eating pizza and drinking soda, it's seriously doubtful that their children will be having chicken, brown rice, and vegetables.

The Shocker

A great number of parents are not good examples when it comes to nutrition. According to the Centers for Disease Control and Prevention (CDC), only 14 percent of adults eat the recommended five or more servings of fruits and vegetables per day. A whopping 35–40 percent of adults regularly skip breakfast. An estimated one-third of the foods consumed by adults in the United States is junk food that is high in sugar, fat, and calories; quick to prepare or purchase; and contains little nutritional value. According to the CDC, more than a third of adults are overweight, and another third are obese. The adults who are leading the way for children are not eating healthy, balanced diets themselves.

The Solution

To help your children overcome their picky eating habits and move on to a lifetime of energy and health, you'll need to set the example. When your little one is refusing to eat the green beans on his plate, she will surely notice if you have eaten yours. Pay attention to the example you're setting and the lessons you're teaching your child. Picky eating is not about making her eat; it's really about teaching her how to make a lifetime of healthy food choices beginning today, one meal at a time.

2

The Fundamental Four

Attitude, Environment, Amounts,
and Rules

The daily battles waged over picky eating can cause parents to lose sight of the big picture and important goals. When you find yourself threatening a stubborn child because he won't eat his broccoli, you may realize that you've become so immersed in the minor skirmishes that you've stopped having any kind of long-term plan and forgotten that eating should be an enjoyable experience. I suggest you step back and take stock of where you are emotionally on the issue; take pen to paper and jot down a few guiding points. Calming your own emotions and making a specific plan will help you guide your child in a truly helpful and joyful way.

The "fundamental four" are essential ideas for creating a healthy eater. They are the guidelines that can get you on the right path so you can get your child on the right path to a lifetime of healthy eating.

1. Attitude: A Good Attitude Is Contagious, so Make Yours Worth Catching

Children are separate human beings from their parents; they have their own opinions and control their own actions. Even when they can barely walk and talk, they have free will. As hard as we may try (and try we do!), we cannot *make* a child eat. Considering that most children eat five or six times a day, it can create major stress in the family when you *do* try to force your child to eat when and what you want. So the first thing to understand is that your job is not to make your child eat, but to present an assortment of healthy options for meals and snacks.

Your attitude about food and mealtime is critical to your child's developing outlook. Even though it may not seem like it at times, your child is constantly watching you and taking life tips from your behavior. It's no surprise that studies have found that parents who don't like vegetables have children who don't like vegetables. It's assumed that these parents don't serve many vegetables and treat them as villains when they do.

One study found that the more a child is lectured about the merits of eating vegetables, the more he assumes they will taste bad and the more he will resist even trying them. This demonstrates that children catch on quickly when parents are trying to sell a behavior they don't truly believe in or follow in their own lives. Conversely, several separate studies by researchers at George Warren Brown School of Social Work and Michigan State University's College of Nursing found that when parents eat more fruits and vegetables, their children do too.

What all this tells us is that before you even begin to address your child's picky eating habits, it would be wise to examine your own habits and attitudes about food. Are you eating a well-balanced diet? Do you get excited about going out to a fast-food restaurant yet treat everyday meals like a chore? Do you find ways to enjoy your vegetables and whole grains every day? Are you a careful grocery shopper, choosing healthy foods in abundance and keeping sweets and junk food to a minimum?

Once you realize that your actions are on display to your child as a prime tool for teaching lifetime beliefs, you can modify your own behavior to set the best example. The side benefit is that you'll be healthier too.

♡ Essential Idea

Attitude is contagious, so make certain that yours conveys a love of healthy food, the ability to choose food wisely, and pleasure in mealtime rituals.

---

2. Environment: What's in Your Kitchen?

A typical family kitchen contains plenty of good, healthy food, along with an assortment of snacks, desserts, and less healthy fare. An adult can sift through the pantry and refrigerator and decide what's best to eat, choosing healthy options for most meals and judiciously choosing the right time for and amount of junk food and desserts. Of course, sometimes adults don't make the right choices, but even when that occurs, they are consciously choosing to forfeit nutritious food for the instant gratification that comes from a less healthy option—but *that* is a topic for a whole other book.

Children, however, lack years of knowledge. They will naturally be drawn to the tastiest option, with no guilt over the resulting choice. They will open the refrigerator or pantry and pick the most appetizing thing they see.

Zoey, two years old

How can you help your child make better choices? The best way is to put the healthy foods where they can be seen easily and allow your child to choose between the nutritious options you present. Place the desserts and junk foods on high shelves or in opaque containers. This way you can dole out the treats when and where you feel they're appropriate.

♡ Essential Idea

Since your child will logically choose to eat the best-tasting foods they can find, make certain the available options are the nutritious foods you most want her to eat.

> **Mother-Speak**
>
> "Our kids were always nagging for cookies and chips, and I was getting terribly frustrated with the daily battles. When you suggested I check my shelves, I realized all the snacks were at perfect child-eye level! I moved them to the very top shelf, and the nagging nearly stopped. Out of sight is out of mind, I guess."
>
> **—Kristina, mother of four-year-old twins Dylan and Leah**

3. Amounts: Providing Proper Portions and Serving Sizes

Part 1 explained the remarkable powers of healthy food and hopefully gave you the inspiration to work to expand your picky eater's menu. Although it presented noteworthy information, it is only common sense that whatever food and drink your child takes in every day will affect him in important ways.

Now that you know about the value of nutritious foods, you may have some new worries. Does your child seem to never eat a full meal? Does dinner mean a few bites of meat, a couple of tablespoons of rice, and four green beans? Does your child always leave half of her food on the plate? Do you wonder how she can have twice the energy you do on such bird-sized meals?

If you're always searching for ideas about how to get your child to eat *more*, the first step may be to take a closer look at what your child is really eating on a daily basis and compare this to actual recommended quantities. There is no exact amount of food necessary for a growing child, as this is affected by each child's size, energy output, previous meals, and other factors. However, we do know that most children's needs fall within a similar range at any particular age.

The first part of your job, then, is to figure out if you really do need to get your little one to eat more food or if you need to change the daily mix and measurements of food groups. It's common for parents to misjudge the serving sizes for their child and assume that she isn't eating enough. What we think of as a miniature serving for ourselves is actually quite large for a child. Your child's stomach is only about the size of her clenched fist; go and look at her hand—it's much smaller than you thought, isn't it? Being portion savvy is a critical part of feeding your child right.

A small toddler needs three-fourths to one cup of vegetables, one-fourth cup of grains, and three tablespoons of meat per *day*, not per meal. That means you spread that amount over all the meals and snacks for the whole day. So a dinnertime serving of vegetables is about a fourth of a cup. That will look like a very small amount to your eye, but it's plenty for your tiny child. A quarter-cup serving of rice is four tablespoons, and a quarter-cup serving of green beans is about four beans!

Typical Daily and Mealtime Serving Sizes

The following charts are intended as a general guide for daily mealtime and snack serving sizes and should be customized for your individual child based on his size, activity level, current growth rate, appetite, and other meals and snacks for the day. Serving sizes are a guideline only, and some children routinely eat more or less than shown, which may be the perfect amount for them. The charts are based on three meals and two snacks per day, so serving sizes should be modified for a different combination.

A child's health, activity, and growth are the most important governing factors for what is the best amount and combination of food per day. If your child is breast-feeding, then breast milk will substitute for some of the calories in all the food groups.

Toddlers (age 18 months to 3 years)
Approximately 1,000 calories daily

Food Group	Foods Included	Daily Total of All Meals and Snacks	Sample Serving per Meal (if divided into 3 meals plus 2 snacks)	Sample Serving per Snack (if divided into 2 snacks plus 3 meals)
Grains	Whole-grain bread, cereal, crackers, pasta, and rice	3 ounces (equivalent)	¾ ounce (one of the following): • ¾ slice of bread • 6 tablespoons pasta, rice, cereal, or oats • 6–12 crackers (depending on size)	⅜ ounce (one of the following): • ¾ of a ½ slice bread • 3 tablespoons pasta, rice, cereal, or oats • 3–6 crackers (depending on size)
Vegetables	All vegetables and 100% vegetable juices	1 cup	¼ cup at each of 3 meals or 6 tablespoons at lunch and at dinner	2 tablespoons
Fruit	All fruits† and 100% fruit juices	1 cup	¼ cup fruit (or ½ cup juice*) at each of 3 meals	2 tablespoons fruit (or ¼ cup juice*)

*No more than ½ cup fruit juice per day is recommended.
†If serving dried fruit, use half the amount of fresh.

Based on information from the U.S. Department of Agriculture (USDA)

(continued)

Toddlers (age 18 months to 3 years) (continued)
Approximately 1,000 calories daily

Food Group	Foods Included	Daily Total of All Meals and Snacks	Sample Serving per Meal (if divided into 3 meals plus 2 snacks)	Sample Serving per Snack (if divided into 2 snacks plus 3 meals)
Milk and Dairy	Milk, yogurt, and cheese	2 cups milk or yogurt or 3 ounces hard cheese or 4 ounces soft cheese	One of the following: • ½ cup milk • ¾ ounce hard cheese • 1 ounce soft cheese	One of the following: • ¼ cup milk • ⅜ ounce hard cheese • ½ ounce soft cheese
Protein	Meat, poultry, fish, eggs, nuts, dry peas and beans (legumes), and soy products	2 ounces (equivalent)	⅔ ounce (1⅓ tablespoons) at each of three meals or 1 ounce (2 tablespoons) at any two meals or ½ egg at each meal	1–2 tablespoons

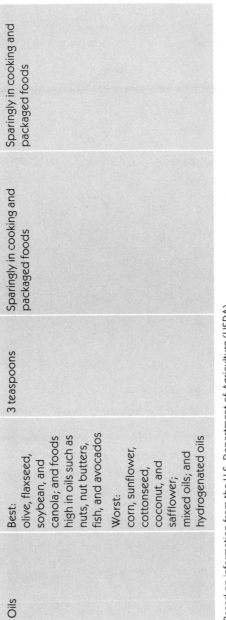

| Oils | Best: olive, flaxseed, soybean, and canola; and foods high in oils such as nuts, nut butters, fish, and avocados | 3 teaspoons | Sparingly in cooking and packaged foods | Sparingly in cooking and packaged foods |
| | Worst: corn, sunflower, cottonseed, coconut, and safflower; mixed oils; and hydrogenated oils | | | |

Based on information from the U.S. Department of Agriculture (USDA)

Preschoolers (age 4 to 8 years)
Approximately 1,200 to 1,400 calories daily

Food Group	Foods Included	Daily Total of All Meals and Snacks	Sample Serving per Meal (if divided into 3 meals plus 2 snacks)	Sample Serving per Snack (if divided into 2 snacks plus 3 meals)
Grains	Whole-grain bread, cereal, crackers, pasta, and rice	4–5 ounces equivalent	Approximately 1–1½ ounces	½ ounce
Vegetables	All vegetables and 100% vegetable juices	1½ cups	⅓ cup at each of 3 meals or 8 tablespoons at lunch and dinner	¼ cup
Fruit	All fruits† and 100% fruit juices	1–1½ cups	¼–⅓ cup fruit (or ½ cup juice*) at each of 3 meals	2 tablespoons–¼ cup fruit (or ¼ cup juice*)

			One of the following:	One of the following:
Milk and Dairy	Milk, yogurt, and cheese	2 cups milk or yogurt or 3 ounces hard cheese or 4 ounces soft cheese	• ½ cup milk or yogurt • ¾ ounce hard cheese • 1 ounce soft cheese	• ¼ cup milk or yogurt • 3/8 ounce hard cheese • ½ ounce soft cheese
Protein	Meat, poultry, fish, eggs, nuts, dry peas and beans (legumes), and soy products	3–4 ounces	¾–1 ounce at each of 3 meals or 1 egg at each meal	1–2 tablespoons

(continued)

*No more than ½ cup fruit juice per day is recommended.
†If serving dried fruit, use half the amount of fresh.

Based on information from the U.S. Department of Agriculture (USDA)

Preschoolers (age 4 to 8 years) (continued)

Approximately 1,200 to 1,400 calories daily

Food Group	Foods Included	Daily Total of All Meals and Snacks	Sample Serving per Meal if divided into 3 meals (plus 2 snacks)	Sample Serving per Snack if divided into 2 snacks (plus 3 meals)
Oils	Best: olive, flaxseed, soybean, and canola; and foods high in oils such as nuts, nut butters, fish, and avocados Worst: corn, sunflower, cottonseed, coconut, and safflower; mixed oils; and hydrogenated oils	4 teaspoons	Sparingly in cooking and packaged foods	Sparingly in cooking and packaged foods

Based on information from the U.S. Department of Agriculture (USDA)

> **♡ Essential Idea**
>
> Monitor your child's food intake based on recommended serving sizes per day and per meal.

4. Rules: Food Rules You Can Break—and Those You Can't

If you've read anything at all about diet and nutrition, I'm sure you've seen all too many "should" and "shouldn'ts." The abundance of rules and dictates can become confusing. I've sorted though the research and data behind some of the typical rules to help you decide if you should follow a particular directive or break it.

Rule: Make family dinnertime a routine.
Verdict: Follow it!
Why? Your children will eat healthier overall, be less likely to abuse alcohol and illicit drugs later in life, and stay closer to you emotionally throughout childhood and perhaps beyond.
Tips: Family mealtime does not have to be formal, structured, or complicated to reap great rewards. A night when you eat sandwiches around the table while chatting about anything under the sun counts just as much as those times when you cook a four-course meal, use your best china, and discuss world affairs.

There are four things that shouldn't be brought to the dinner table: lectures, reprimands, rigid expectations, and demands for specific conversation.

The key to success for the family dinner idea is regularity—four to five times a week or more. Infrequent family dinners tend to be uncomfortable, stressed, or mundane. However, families that make a practice of dining together in a relaxed, pleasant atmosphere reap the most benefits. When sitting around the table is a familiar event, your children will naturally open up about things that are going on in their lives—or in their heads. They'll absorb more of the lessons you hope to impart about healthy eating and healthy values through the casual, regular dinner atmosphere.

Rule: Set your child's meals to occur at the same time every day.
Verdict: Break it!
Why? Eating by the clock teaches your child to ignore her bodily cues.
Tips: It's great to have a set but flexible schedule for mealtimes. For example, eat breakfast "after we get up and get dressed"; eat lunch "around noon"; and eat dinner "soon after Mom gets home from work." But it's also permissible for your child *not* to be hungry exactly when you're ready to serve a meal. His level of hunger should not be taken as a sign of disrespect or lack of appreciation for your cooking skills, but rather as a healthy sign of listening to his own hunger cues.

Many things affect how hungry your child is at any given moment, but the time on the clock is not one of them. His hunger level is affected by how long it's been since his last meal, how active he has been, what types of food and drink he last consumed, his energy level, his blood sugar level, his hormones, his internal rhythms, and his health.

What's more important than a rigid schedule for meals and snacks is helping your child tune in to his body signals so that he eats according to his actual physical needs for food and drink. This means the second important part of this rule is to avoid non-nutritive snacking that fills your child up and to provide nutritious options (such as leftovers from a meal) for the times when he is hungry.

Koda, fifteen months old

Rule: Eat an apple a day.
Verdict: Follow it!
Why? An apple a day really will help keep the doctor away.
Tips: Apples are easy to serve, easy to eat, rich in nutrients, high in antioxidants, and a great source of fiber. Making apples a part of your child's daily diet can help build stronger bones, boost heart health, decrease levels of low-density lipoprotein (LDL, or "bad cholesterol"), prevent diabetes, and reduce the risk of asthma and cancer. Apples even help keep breath fresh and teeth white!

While an apple a day is great, three servings of apple products weekly still reap these benefits. Organic, unwaxed apples are best, when you can get them. Diced apple added to other foods, applesauce, natural pulp-retained apple juice, dried apples, and even a low-sugar apple cobbler all bring outstanding health benefits.

Rule: Eat until you are full.
Verdict: Break it!
Why? Once your child realizes that she is full, she probably was already full several bites ago. The feeling of being full can sometimes be delayed or disguised by outside influences.
Tips: The feeling of "fullness" is not an instantaneous sensation; it gradually builds as we eat and adjusts as food moves through our body. External signals, such as how good the food tastes, how quickly we eat, and other distractions during mealtime, can interfere with reading signs of fullness. In one study at New Mexico State University, children were asked how they "knew they were full." Most cited the external cue of when their plates were empty—a terrible way to judge!

If you discover that your child is not in sync with her body cues, you can help her out. Put smaller servings on her plate, and if she wants more food, ask helpful questions such as "Are you feeling hungry, or was it really tasty?" In addition, make it a rule to wait ten or fifteen minutes before second helpings or dessert to determine whether she's really still hungry. Most children will find that a pause allows them time to tune in to their body's hunger and fullness sensations.

Rule: Clean your plate.
Verdict: Break it!
Why? Babies are born with natural appetite control. They eat when they're hungry and stop when they've had enough. As they

Professional-Speak

"[People] are more influenced by their environment than whether they are actually still hungry. Since most of the signals in our society, from TV commercials to our best friends, tell us to 'eat, eat, eat,' it can be difficult to control intake if we're ignoring our own bodies."

—**Brian Wansink, Ph.D., author of** *Mindless Eating: Why We Eat More Than We Think*

grow into childhood, they begin to eat for reasons other than hunger: the food tastes good, it looks appetizing, others are eating, it's lunchtime, or Mommy and Daddy told them to eat. The problem with all of these reasons is that a child loses the ability to hear the natural communication of his body signals and begins to eat according to outside forces. A fascinating study to prove how dangerous it is to turn off your natural-born appetite control system was completed by Brian Wansink, Ph.D., director of Cornell University Food and Brand Lab. He created a bottomless soup bowl that refilled itself as people ate and invited groups of unsuspecting people to lunch. People in the comparison group who ate from normal bowls consumed just over ten ounces of soup. The bottomless soup bowl eaters consumed anywhere from fifteen ounces to more than a quart of soup! Dr. Wansink calls this "mindless eating," and it's something we want to prevent in our children—which means the "clean your plate club" should be closed for good.

In addition to disturbing a child's natural appetite regulators, many parents misjudge the appropriate serving sizes for their children, piling a nearly adult-sized serving on a child's dinner plate—

Lilly, nineteen months old

another version of the bottomless soup bowl. A child's stomach is about the size of his clenched fist, which is too darn small for an adult-sized serving.

Tips: To get a better idea of appropriate serving sizes for your child, refer to the food charts provided earlier. Keep in mind that the charts are only a gauge that you need to customize daily for every meal and snack. Your child's hunger level will be tied to a variety of factors: when he last ate, what types and amount of food he ate last, how much exercise he's had, how much sleep he's had, where he is in his growth curve, and possibly other factors as well.

Mother-Speak

"I bought my son a separated toddler dish with sections labeled for the different food groups. Not only does he love it because it keeps all his food from touching (a major no-no!), I realized that it helps me give him the right amount of each type of food."

—**Nadine, mother of three-year-old Owen**

Rule: Never let your child eat in front of the TV.

Verdict: Break it!

Why? What? No popcorn with the movie?

Tips: Not eating in front of the TV makes good sense because it's easy to lose track of how much food your child eats when you're both distracted by the program you're watching. However, most people find it enjoyable to snack while watching a movie. Therefore, a better option than banning this practice altogether is to make a plan in advance. Put your chosen serving for each person in an individual bowl or on his or her plate, or make it fun by filling a muffin tray with various snacks. Then encourage the kids to slowly enjoy their treat while they watch.

Rule: Make sure your child's diet is nutritionally balanced at every meal.

Verdict: Break it!

Why? It's nearly impossible to feed any child three balanced meals every day, let alone make a picky eater achieve this lofty goal. Furthermore, it's not necessary to make every meal perfect for your child to achieve a healthy diet.

Of course, it would be best to eat as healthfully as possible at every meal, every day. Realistically, though, this is impossible, and it would be stress-provoking to even try. Children's appetites change frequently—day to day, and even hour to hour. Just like adults, sometimes they'll be drawn to one food over another, and they may fill up on one dish without taking a bite from the rest. In addition, it's perfectly human to eat high-calorie, low-nutrient foods occasionally. The key is to limit treats and have a plan and family rules so that every meal doesn't automatically come with dessert, and every television session isn't accompanied by a bag of chips. Treats are a fun and normal part of life, just not too often and not too much.

Tips: Pay attention to the balance of your child's daily and weekly meals and snacks. Look at the big picture of her eating habits rather than obsessing about every morsel at every meal. For instance, a meal that consists only of raw veggies and dip with a slice of whole-grain toast may be short on protein. But you can make it up easily at the next meal or snack.

Rule: Don't let your child eat food directly from the bag, box, or jar.

Verdict: Follow it!

Why? They'll eat way too much.

Professional-Speak

"I tell people to eat as well as possible during the week, but to eat favorite foods in moderation on Saturdays. This model gives people something to look forward to and seems to help them stick to healthy eating habits."

—**Stephen Ball, Ph.D., associate professor of exercise physiology, University of Missouri**

Tips: Whether it's a bag of chips, a box of crackers, or a jar of olives, eating directly from the package blurs the perceived amount eaten, and most kids (and adults) end up consuming a supersized serving. Check the serving size on the package, consider your child's daily and weekly diet, and make a choice of how much is appropriate. Put this on a plate or in a bowl, and don't allow an immediate second helping. Encourage your child to wait twenty minutes or so after eating before going back for more, since it takes awhile for his system to register fullness.

Rule: No snacks right before bed.
Verdict: Break it!
Why? A prebedtime snack keeps blood sugar levels consistent, can help your child fall asleep, and prevents hunger from waking her too early.
Tips: Our digestive systems slow down at night, so eating a big meal before bed can make it hard for a child to fall asleep, but feeling hungry can keep her awake, disrupt her sleep, or cause her to wake too early the next morning. The best choice is to provide a small, low-sugar snack with a healthy dose of carbohydrates and minimal protein about thirty minutes to an hour before bedtime. Here are a few ideas for prebedtime snacks:

- An English muffin with low-sugar jam
- Oatmeal with bananas
- Whole-grain, low-sugar cereal and milk
- A bagel (especially whole wheat) with cheese or turkey
- Whole-grain crackers with tuna
- Low-sugar oatmeal cookies with warm milk
- Wheat pretzels with string cheese
- Whole-wheat toast or apple slices with natural peanut butter

- Brown rice pudding
- Yogurt and low-sugar granola

Providing a healthy evening snack is a good idea. Just be sure your child eats it because she's hungry and not out of habit. And be sure to have her brush her teeth after that evening snack!

Rule: Avoid fast-food restaurants.

Verdict: Follow it!

Why? Yale University's Rudd Center for Food Policy and Obesity analyzed 3,039 meal combinations from twelve fast-food chains. Only 12 of those meal combinations were considered nutritious for preschoolers; 99.6 percent were *not* nutritious. Only 15 meals met nutrition criteria for older kids, meaning 99.5 percent lacked adequate nutrition for that age group.

When the researchers examined menu items that were advertised for children, they found that 30 percent or more of the calories were from sugar and saturated fat and filled with at least half of

Hannah, one year old

a child's daily recommended amount of sodium. It's likely that the few meal combinations that were considered nutritious were actually those that included apple slices or other options kids hardly ever eat at a fast-food restaurant.

The study also confirmed what parents already know: fast-food marketers target children across a variety of media. The average preschooler sees three ads a day for fast-food restaurants, so it's no surprise that 40 percent of children ask their parents for this type of food at least once a week, while 15 percent nag daily. Eighty-four percent of parents with young children give in to that request at least once a week.

Tips: Every once in a while a fast-food junk meal is fine, but most families hit these restaurants too frequently. If you go out to eat often, try not to present going out for fast food as a *treat* but rather as an opportunity for a healthy *meal* away from home. Almost all restaurants have healthy choices on the menu, but it takes time and thoughtfulness to order them. Plan ahead if you can; most restaurant chains have online menus you can view in advance. Set rules about choices. For example, allow your child to pick one unhealthy item; so if she gets french fries, she must get milk or water to drink rather than soda or a shake.

Rule: It's okay to break the rules once in a while.
Verdict: Follow it!
Why? Parenting is a complicated and challenging job. There are many facets to the daily efforts required to raise children. On top of that, parents and children are human beings. You cannot be 100 percent responsible for every action your child takes. From a very young age, his own decisions affect his behavior. No parent—no matter how dedicated—can follow a child around all day, every day, and monitor every morsel of food that goes into his mouth. To even attempt that level of control would drive both parent and child crazy, and it would likely backfire into a serious battle of wills.

Alex, three years old

Set your rules to build good habits, since long-term thinking reaps lifelong rewards. Convincing your child to eat a green bean should be about more than that one bean, because it actually represents all the future green beans in his life. Instead of always being focused on one particular meal or the snack of the moment, try to think about each event as an opportunity to teach your child healthy attitudes toward food and eating and to build good habits for today and the future.

Tips: Make sure you create family rules thoughtfully. Pick your battles wisely—and when you pick one, be sure you win!

3

Tips, Tricks, and Tactics

....

Solving Picky Eater Problems

Picky eating is common in the early childhood years, but children are unique in their approach to pickiness. Parents must deal with a variety of issues that fall under the picky eating umbrella. There isn't one perfect solution that works for every issue or for every child.

Even siblings can be very different from one another. I have four children who are as alike as apples, oranges, spaghetti, and sushi. It often amazes me that they were birthed by the same parents and raised in the same home. They are distinctive individuals and have widely diverse food preferences. I have one child who is an adventurous eater—he's tried octopus, buffalo, alligator, and chocolate-covered grasshoppers. He begs me to buy the most unusual-looking fruits and vegetables at the farmers market just so he can try them. He loves ethnic food and is up for any unique food experience; he even picked a dim sum restaurant in our local international district for his birthday breakfast. I have another child who has an extremely limited number of foods he'll eat, right down to the specific brand of orange juice he has every morning. He'd truly rather skip a meal than eat something that's not on his preferred list. We raised both boys the same way, which demonstrates that personality plays a large part in a child's eating style.

When we expect all children to act exactly the same or the same child to respond precisely the same way in every situation (which they don't), we set ourselves up for frustration. It's important for us to have a wide repertoire of parenting tools, so we can modify what we do to make it work best for each child in our family and in each different situation.

Top Ten Tips, Tricks, and Tactics

What you'll find in Part 3 is a handful of the most common food-related problems that occur during early childhood, along with a variety of solutions for each issue. The best advice I can give you is to be flexible. Look through the lists of solutions and choose those that make the most sense for you and for the child involved.

The selection of solutions for each problem varies. I don't mean for you to follow every suggestion as if it were a road map. These ideas are meant to act as starting points for you to develop your own customized solution. With this in mind, the following sections provide you with a number of practical solutions for solving each type of picky eating problem.

When you are struggling with an issue, review your options based on material found throughout this book and other sources as well, and consider your child's personality, your parenting style, and your family goals. Then put your decision into action. If your original plan doesn't bring success (and often it won't), then try another option—and, on occasion, even a third option until you feel good about how things are going. Raising children is a complicated job, and there is rarely a concise answer to any problem. Try to relax along the way; picky eating problems are never solved in a day. Keep your eye on the future and your long-term goals, and celebrate little victories along your path.

When you decide which particular solutions you'll be using, write them down on a piece of paper. You might want to tack it up on the refrigerator to help you remember the details. Discuss

Kadence, fourteen months old

your plan with other adults who spend time with your child. View your plan as a general guide to the next month or two rather than as a rigid, set-in-stone rulebook. After all, your child will be eating for the rest of her life, so taking a few months to instill new habits is really a blink of an eye compared to a lifetime of good eating habits. Think back to your own childhood and your teen years—chances are you were not eating even half as well as you are now. You've learned a lot about nutrition over the years, and your child will learn too. Think of your efforts today as training camp for your child's independent lifetime of eating.

The good news here is that if you are making an effort to improve your child's diet and eating behavior, then chances are very good you will succeed. It won't be immediate and it won't be perfection, but by paying attention and using some creative tips and solutions, you will definitely see improvements and be well on your way to raising a child with healthy eating habits.

1. Let Long-Term Goals Be Your Guide

Any one meal or even a whole day of meals won't make or break your plan, so relax a bit. Set long-term goals for eating habits, and use them as your guide. Modify your approach from one of trying to have total control over every single bite your child takes to being the overseer of your child's weekly nutritional intake.

Goals that are too grand can be hard to adhere to, so make some minigoals along the way. For example, if your child eats no vegetables at all right now, don't make it a goal for him to have five servings a day right off; instead, begin by including one vegetable daily at dinner. After a time, perhaps a week or even a month, increase the goal to one vegetable at dinner plus one at lunch. Work your way up to making vegetables a regular part of your child's daily meals. Your *actual goal* is to create good lifetime habits—and you can't do that overnight. Be realistic: don't expect perfection from your child or yourself.

2. Make Small Changes to Reap Big Results

It can be hard—almost impossible, sometimes—to change your child's rigidly held eating habits. Instead of trying to overhaul every meal and snack, begin by making a few small changes, one at a time, toward a more nutritious diet. Pick just a few items to start with. Once these become routine, then change another couple of items. If you follow this process, you'll find that within a year you will have improved your child's overall diet significantly.

Following are some ideas for some small changes you can make; experiment with them until you find substitutes that your child will accept willingly:

- Replace soda with homemade lemonade or a flavored water drink, then over time, begin to substitute plain water as the main beverage.
- Substitute high-fat beef or pork sausages, hot dogs, or lunch meats with similar versions made of turkey, chicken, or soy.
- Instead of nonnutritious snacks, chips, or crackers, try pita and hummus, whole-grain pretzels with peanut butter, or veggie sticks with dip.
- Add a healthy side dish to a typical meal. Raw vegetables, applesauce, mixed fruit, or a serving of yogurt can share the plate with everyday favorites.
- Add sliced fruit, berries, or chopped nuts to a favorite cereal or oatmeal.
- Serve the same foods as usual, but modify the portion sizes to increase the healthy foods and decrease the less nutritious ones. Slightly increase the amount of lean proteins, vegetables, and whole grains, and slightly decrease the servings of less healthy foods and desserts.
- Slowly reduce the amount of salt, sugar, butter, cheese, and oil that you use in preparing food. Your child won't notice small changes, and you can gradually move toward using much less of these ingredients.

3. Don't Shock Your Kids—Gradually Transform Them

It would create chaos if you suddenly eliminated your child's regular foods and replaced them with healthy options: your picky eater might become a noneater! Instead, examine your child's favorite foods and make subtle changes to create healthier versions. By making small adjustments over time, your child's taste buds will adjust until you can finally replace the old version with a healthier alternative. Following are examples of some common favorites and tips for making the switch.

Macaroni and Cheese

Original: White macaroni and powder-based cheese sauce

The Switch: Slowly replace the macaroni with whole-wheat pasta; first with one-fourth whole wheat to three-fourths white. After a few meals, make it half-and-half, working toward a full serving of whole wheat. Once the pasta has been transformed, you can move on to replacing the other ingredients, one at a time. For example, use two-thirds of the powdered cheese sauce and one-third real low-fat cheese, working up to half-and-half and then all real cheese. Then move on to changing from whole milk to nonfat and reducing or eliminating the butter from the recipe.

Peanut Butter and Jelly Sandwich

Original: White bread with sugar-based jelly and processed peanut butter containing sugar and hydrogenated oil

The Switch: Begin by replacing one slice of bread with whole wheat, keeping the other slice white. Place the sandwich on the plate with the white bread on top. Over time, experiment with replacing both pieces of white bread with whole-wheat bread. The next step is to change to one-half sugar-based jelly and one-half fruit-only spread, working up to 100 percent fruit-only spread. After you've accomplished a switch of the bread and jelly, replace a portion of the processed peanut butter with a low-sugar, non–trans fat version, gradually changing completely to the low-sugar choice. Make these subtle adjustments over a period of several months so your child has a chance to adjust to the flavor changes over time.

Breakfast Cereal

Original: A non-nutritious, sugary breakfast cereal

The Switch: Begin by adding a spoonful of a healthier cereal (higher in fiber, lower in sugar) to your child's bowl. Over time, increase the amount of the better cereal to one-third, while reducing the sugary type to two-thirds. You can help the process along by adding fresh fruit to the bowl. Build toward a mixture of half

Chase, two years old

sugary cereal and half of the healthier variety; keep increasing the percentage until your child has a new standard breakfast cereal. It may help to pick a replacement cereal that has a similar shape and texture to the old standby. Explore the cereal aisle, and you'll find an amazing number of healthy choices from which to choose.

Cookies
Original: High-sugar, high-fat, store-bought cookies or cookies made from a packaged mix
The Switch: Lots of kids love cookies, and you'd be amazed to find that they will accept those with healthier ingredients just as easily as the more sugar-filled choices. If you bake your own cookies, then you can slowly replace individual ingredients with better choices, such as substituting whole-wheat flour for white flour and carob chips for chocolate chips.

Alternatively, it may be easier to go for an entirely different type of cookie than trying to modify your child's favorites; if you try to substitute a favorite with an organic, low-fat distant cousin, your child might turn up his nose. Instead try something entirely different—give your chocolate chip lover an oatmeal raisin cookie instead. When purchasing premade cookies, shop for those that contain less sugar and are free from trans fat and artificial additives.

4. Teach, Don't Preach

Change your vocabulary: eliminate unpleasant words, such as *diet* and *junk*, when referring to food. Avoid outdated negatively phrased demands, such as "If you don't finish dinner, you can't have dessert." Rephrase your comments to be more meaningful, such as, "Once you've had your healthy foods, if you're still hungry, then you can have dessert." Avoid labeling a particular food *bad* or *good*; instead, discuss the properties of the food and what it does or doesn't do for your health. Don't lecture your child about eating too much junk food when she's halfway though a bag of chips; it does no good at that point, except to tire you both of the speech.

Avoid using food, particularly sweets and treats, as a reward, punishment, or source of comfort for pain or sadness. Try not to give food the main spotlight at family gatherings or parties, and focus on the joy and fun of people being together. You'll want your child to learn to savor and appreciate good food, but as part of the entire social experience.

Teaching your child about nutrition is a daily journey best traveled in short segments. Take your time, and keep your eye on long-term goals.

5. When Necessary, Be Sneaky

Even after you've set your long-term goals and minigoals, after you've begun to make simple changes and teach your little one about proper nutrition, you still have a long way to go before healthy eating becomes second nature to your child. In the meantime, it doesn't hurt to sneak some healthy ingredients into your everyday recipes. Find compatible colors and flavors, or add a mild-tasting vegetable to a more flavorful mix. Part 4 contains several recipes by the master Sneaky Chef, Missy Chase Lapine. Here are a few other ideas to get you started:

Add this:	To this:
Chopped spinach, mashed carrots, and minced zucchini, celery, or onion	Hamburger patties or meat loaf
Pureed carrots, finely chopped peppers, or tofu	Spaghetti sauce
Whole-wheat flour, ground flax, wheat germ, dates, nuts, or raisins	Cookie dough
Oat bran, ground flax, apples, bananas, or berries	Pancakes or muffins
Sweet potatoes or pureed squash or carrots	Macaroni and cheese
Mashed cauliflower or pureed chickpeas	Mashed potatoes
Cottage cheese, yogurt, nuts, seeds, and fruit	Oatmeal or cereal
Pureed or finely chopped vegetables, such as bell peppers, cauliflower, and carrots (either on top or hidden in the sauce), whole-wheat crust, or crust made with ground flax	Pizza
Finely chopped or pureed green beans, carrots, zucchini, cabbage, peas, or squash	Ramen noodles
Finely chopped zucchini, cauliflower, pea pods, peppers, zucchini, mushrooms, and tomatoes	Soup or stew

Mixing a few hidden ingredients into recipes can boost the nutrients in any meal. It is a great way to provide healthy, wholesome food while your child's taste buds mature. At the same time, continue to introduce new foods in a less stressful manner. Hidden additions are a great way to provide nutrients while your child is in the process of learning how to eat right.

Once your child tastes a meal that contains hidden ingredients and enjoys it, you might even choose to state matter-of-factly that the macaroni and cheese contains squash and carrots, as if it's no big deal. This allows your child to view the ingredients with a whole new eye ("Wow, who knew squash could taste so good?"). It may even make it easier for him to try squash the next time you serve it by itself.

Professional-Speak

"You should continue to serve healthy foods and encourage your kids to try them. As a Sneaky Chef, the struggle to get your kids to eat those foods will become less urgent. With that in mind, why not start sneaking around your kitchen tonight?"

—Missy Chase Lapine, author of _The Sneaky Chef_

6. Choose Wise Rules

Sure, it would be great to ban fast food, sugar, and soda from your child's life and never have her question the rule. And it would be fantastic simply to tell her to eat five servings of vegetables per day and have it be so. However, TV commercials, friends' homes, the movie theater, class parties, grandparents, and a zillion other situations will put unhealthy delights in front of your child on a daily basis. Add to that the fact that many children are naturally antivegetable, and any parent has a full-time job battling outside influences.

Dictating a litany of food rules isn't the answer, though. Studies tell us that parents who impose too-strict rules about eating can end up with children who are extremely fussy eaters or who become overeaters. The right answer is likely to be a few thoughtful, practical, and important rules tempered by common sense.

While every family is unique, some nutritional basics apply to all children. So think about what's important to you and which issues need the most guidance. Here are two sample rules—and the reasoning behind them—to get you thinking about what your own food guidelines should be:

- **You can have one treat a day.** Many families find the "one treat a day" rule—or the more ambitious "one treat a week" rule—much easier to enforce than forbidding treats altogether. If you create this sort of rule, though, make sure that you are clear what you mean by "treats." Is a whole-wheat pretzel a treat? Are french fries a treat? Is a can of soda a treat? Once you get the specifics down, this rule can be a lifesaver; each time your child wants a sweet or chips, you can ask, "Is this your one treat today?" Asking this helpful question can help her learn how to make more thoughtful food choices.

- **You must try two bites before saying you don't like something.** When you pile up a new food on your child's plate, it can be an immediate turnoff and shift his opposition into high gear. So instead of giving him a full serving of something new, just put a tablespoon or so on the plate and require a two-bite "tasting" to see how he likes the new food. I don't suggest a one-bite rule because one small bite can go down so fast your child barely tastes the food. Two bites might be just enough to break down his resistance and give him the actual flavor. If he finds that it's better than he thought, it might open his mind to the idea of new foods and get him to explore some new culinary horizons. If it doesn't get him to eat what you're offering, at least you'll have many chances to introduce new things over time.

7. Create Smart Habits

Kids are naturally wired to follow daily routines and rituals. Whatever they do every day, they will continue to do every day. So work hard to instill some great eating habits. Once they're established, you'll find your child automatically following these patterns. Here are a few sample food routines to consider. These ideas can get you thinking about your own family's routines:

- Eat breakfast every day. One step better—eat something from each food group at breakfast: grains, fruit or vegetable, dairy, and protein.
- Fruit or vegetables are the go-to snack if you are hungry before a meal.
- Sugary desserts (like ice cream sundaes, cake, or pie) are rare but wonderful experiences, typically for special occasions like birthdays, vacations, or holidays.
- Lunch and dinner always include at least one vegetable.
- Added butter, sugar, ketchup, syrups, and sauces are used in small doses.
- Soda pop is a rarely served beverage, perhaps reserved for parties or dining out.
- Water is on the table at every meal.

These are examples of great lifetime habits, since they are all based on sound nutritional theories. Decide which of them you are going to adopt in your family, and add some of your own as well. Remember, kids learn best by example, so be the leader.

8. Make Food and Mealtime Fun

Mealtime is a great time to enjoy being with your family. It should be as much about togetherness as it is about the food on the table. For many busy families, it's one of the few times that everyone can sit down together and interact without interruption. Remember to take pleasure in this special time.

Be adventurous! Experiment with colors, shapes, textures, and the presentation of food. If the meat is the highlight of the meal and a pile of green beans sits off in the corner, it's unlikely that the beans will command your child's attention. But sauté the beans with olive oil, garlic, ginger, and low-sodium soy sauce (or olive oil, dill, and leeks), and they just might grab her interest. Adding a new twist to a common food also has the added benefit of introducing her to new flavors.

The dinner table is not the time for serious or unpleasant conversations nor for hashing through the problems of the day. Keep table talk light and happy so that mealtime is a time of family joy and camaraderie.

Expect and prompt good table manners, but don't be a nag about the little things. Table manners are best taught in bite-sized pieces over a year or more. Be relaxed but consistent in what you expect, and display your own good manners when reminding your children to use theirs.

9. Encourage Independence

You won't always be with your child at meals or snack time. So set him up for success for those times when you two aren't in the

Will, three years old

same room. You can do this by creating routines, as mentioned earlier.

You can also engage your child's decision-making skills by offering choices from several healthy options. For example, ask if he'd like his carrots raw or cooked, or if he'd prefer rice or pasta. If your child is older, provide him with general guidelines and then set him free to work within them; for example, allow him to pack his

> **Father-Speak**
>
> "Once a month we let our kids plan and prepare a simple meal. They discuss the menu, help us shop, and are in charge of the kitchen. Whatever they make, they eat—and they have a great time doing it."
>
> **—Aaron, father of ten-year-old Sophie,**
>
> **eight-year-old Andrew, and seven-year-old Julia**

own lunch but give him a checklist of the types of foods it must contain, such as one fruit, a whole grain, and a protein.

When you can, allow your child to help prepare meals and snacks, since hands-on participation will create a more realistic connection to the lessons you are teaching about food choices.

10. Be a Good Example

It's easier to teach how to eat healthily when you are leading the way with your own food choices. Even if it's not always evident, your child learns most about healthy eating habits from watching what you put on your plate and in your mouth. If you show her that fruit makes a great snack, vegetables are enjoyable, and sweets are to be savored in small and infrequent servings, she might just follow your lead.

Common Questions and Practical Solutions

You can use the general rules and ideas we've already covered in this book as a guide to help your picky eater become a healthy eater. What follows are a number of specific questions and concerns that my test parent group brought to the table. The solutions provided will give you the tools and ideas you need to handle everyday food issues in your own family.

Picky-Proofing Your Baby or Toddler

Our four-year-old son is an extremely picky eater. Is there any way to prevent our eighteen-month-old baby from being as picky as his brother?

As you learned in Part 1, it's not possible to change your child's food preferences entirely, and some picky eating habits are based on biology. However, there are a number of things you can do to help your baby accept more food choices from the start. You can also modify your own actions to begin to establish habits and routines that will "picky-proof" your child as he gets a bit older. I'll throw some ideas your way, but keep in mind that you won't use them all—and even those you do follow may only work some of the time. However, all of the following ideas are steps to healthy eating, so there's no harm in giving them a try:

• Watch the food habits your baby is forming. Work hard to instill good practices and avoid building unhealthy habits. For example, if your child loves fresh fruit for breakfast, make sure there's always some in the house so he'll come to expect this as part of his first meal of the day. If he loves to munch on whole-grain cereal bits while you are shopping, avoid introducing him to the free cookie that is often offered in grocery store bakeries. In addition, avoid practices such as including a sweet dessert after every meal or serving lunch in front of the television, since your baby will quickly come to expect these as standard mealtime events.

• Avoid using food as a pacifier, a prize, or a disciplinary tool. Don't offer food as a way to stop your baby from fussing or as a soother for times when he is scared or hurt. Avoid promising sweets as a bribe for good behavior or taking away dessert for bad behavior. It's best to keep food in its natural place and not give it power over your child's actions, as this will set both of you up for a lifetime pattern of food battles and emotionally fueled eating.

• Serve small portions on small plates so your child isn't overwhelmed. A huge plate of food can be a big turnoff to a young child. In addition, a large plate can prevent you from accurately assessing the proper portion amount, so your child may be forced to eat more than he needs. Allow requests for second helpings of healthy foods, and don't make a big deal about food that is left on the plate.

• Do a taste test before serving. Before you offer something new to your baby, taste it first! Make sure it is fresh and tasty. An accidental offering of a spoiled or unpleasant food can turn your baby off trying similar foods for a long time.

• Casually introduce many new foods. Studies show that the window of time between six months and two years of age is the best time to expose children to a wide variety of foods, since toddler pickiness has not yet set in. Right from the start, offer your baby lots of different foods, always in small servings at first. Continue to offer a food over time, even if your baby isn't interested, since the regular sight and smell of a food is the first step to his becoming accustomed to it. It can take a great many exposures before he will be willing to taste something new, but each exposure takes you closer, so keep trying.

• Keep mealtime relaxed. The eating environment should be as stress-free as possible. Joyful mealtimes help babies start off with a positive experience of the dinner table that wards off food battles in the future. If your baby is a frequent witness to food battles between you and his older brother or sister, he may follow in those footsteps.

• Don't pressure your child to eat something he doesn't like. If your baby turns his head away or makes a disgusted face, don't make him eat any more of the food at that sitting. Give him something else that you know he enjoys. This will set the stage for him to be open to trying new foods, since he'll know you will respect his wishes, and thus he'll be more likely to feel that eating is a pleasant, unpressured experience.

• Avoid giving your baby too many choices. If you offer a menu of choices for every meal and every snack, your child will quickly become used to this. If you offer up too many options now, you'll spend the next fifteen years as your child's personal chef.

• Show your own enjoyment of a variety of healthy foods. Children learn from observation, and they pick up cues about what is good to eat from watching adults. Be sure your baby is a part of your dining experience so that he can learn from watching you.

Determine if Your Child Is Eating Enough

I try to serve my child the right food, but lots of it ends up on the floor or as a pile of mush on her plate. Plus, I'm not always with her, so I can't be sure what she's eating all day, every day. How do I know if my child is getting enough food?

It would be impossible to monitor every bite that actually makes it to your child's tummy, and it would be severely stress-inducing even to try!

If your health care provider tells you that your child is healthy and within the normal range for height and weight, then she is likely getting enough to eat. Keep in mind that some children are normally slim, and simply being on the low end of the growth charts isn't necessarily a cause for concern.

Rather than the simple question of whether your child is eating enough food, the more important question is whether she is getting the adequate calories and nutrition for optimal health and growth, since children can grow and thrive even with a substandard diet. There can be problems, though, even if they are not currently obvious. For one, a child who gets by without the best nutrition won't maximize her growth and development. Lack of proper nutrition can also affect how well she learns. Continued poor nutrition can eventually begin to erode your child's health, and because children are so resilient, you may not realize she is nutritionally deficient until health problems begin to crop up.

If you have a light eater on your hands and are concerned that she doesn't get enough nutrition from her food, here are a few tips to help you be sure that she gets enough calories in the form of the balanced nutrition she needs:

• Provide meals that are richer in nutrients so she can have smaller servings, such as a peanut butter and jelly sandwich—made with whole-grain bread; natural, non–trans fat peanut butter; and no-sugar fruit spread—or bean and brown rice tostadas with tomato salsa, made with corn tortillas.

• Don't let your child fill up on liquid calories, even if they are healthy juice drinks. Fluids take up the stomach space needed for healthful foods that provide more fiber and an assortment of vitamins.

• Don't permit your child to fill up on low-calorie favorites, such as grapes or strawberries. Although these are healthy foods and provide fiber and bulk, they also provide fewer calories and contain quite a bit of natural sugar, so they are best in smaller doses. If your little one fills up with them, she won't have room for other types of food to round out her diet.

• Limit snacking on foods such as crackers, pretzels, or dry cereal that may curb your child's appetite at the next meal. If she is hungry before mealtime, try giving her a small serving of veggies and dip, or pita and hummus, that can be counted as part of her meal. Better yet, serve one part of the meal early as an appetizer so she'll get a balanced meal, even though it is eaten in several courses.

• If you have a child who resists sitting down to a meal, change the presentation. Provide the same food, but call it a snack instead of a meal, and serve it casually. You might even throw a blanket on the floor and call it a picnic.

• Be certain that your child eats frequently—about five or six times a day. Stick to healthy choices, of course, for both meals and snacks.

Pick the Right Battles and Then Win the Ones You Pick

It seems like mealtime has become a major war in our house. From morning until night, food issues dominate our household. Help!

The vast majority of picky eating problems are not life-threatening, so it's rare that an issue warrants a full-out war. Most children will respond to the ideas and solutions presented in this book, but it is never a one-day, immediate change. Improvement takes time and patience. It is important, of course, to continue to work with your child, but a picky eating issue is seldom worth a daily war. So take a deep breath and consider these tips:

• Your child is likely eating better than you think. Check out the food charts in Part 2 to get a better idea of what a typical meal and snack should look like. It might help to keep a food log for a day or two to chart exactly what your child eats and compare the two so you have the facts. If you see problem areas, such as a lack in a certain food category, then you can make specifically targeted changes.

• Some aspects of picky eating should rightfully be ignored. For example, if your child adores green beans and zucchini but won't go near broccoli, then serve him green beans and zucchini for a while and reintroduce broccoli in the future. However, if your child shuns all green vegetables in favor of white pasta, getting him to eat some green is a battle worth fighting.

• Instead of filling your child's plate with what you think he should eat, try serving meals family-style. Fill serving bowls or platters with various foods and give your child an empty plate. Allow him to pick and choose from what's there. Of course, since they are all healthy foods, it doesn't really matter which ones he picks. Don't offer an entire assortment of new or unusual foods that your child will likely avoid. Stick to familiar dishes with one or two new items at each meal. When a child fills his own plate, he'll be more likely to eat what he's selected.

• Your main job right now is to provide a variety of healthy foods that includes all the food groups and to limit sweets, soda, foods that contain trans fat, and junk food. It's also your job to begin to teach your child about food choices so that when you're not around, such as when he enters school, he'll have the basics to guide his choices. It's important for you to help your child begin a healthy relationship with eating. You'll want him to enjoy his meals and learn to eat the appropriate types and amounts of food based on what his body needs rather than on exterior signals such as emotions, social environment, or the mere proximity of food.

Stay Consistent

> I really get tired of making custom meals for my kids every day, but when I prepare a balanced dinner and demand that they eat what's in front of them, they whine and fuss and complain. They barely eat at all! So sometimes I end up making them boxed macaroni and cheese, because I can't let them starve, can I?

First of all, don't worry so much. If your kids miss a meal by choice, they *won't* starve. They'll just be hungry and fill up at the next meal or snack. The irony here is that while parents stress out and fret because children miss a meal, those same children get down from the dinner table and take off to play without giving the situation a moment's thought—until an hour or two later when they actually feel hungry. Then they'll be back in the kitchen looking for something to eat.

It may seem that giving in with their favorite food is better than nothing, but that's not the case. The reality here is that when your children won't eat the fish, rice, and broccoli you've prepared, and you give in and provide macaroni and cheese (for the fifth day in a row), you are substituting a healthy meal packed full of vitamins, minerals, and nutrients with a plate full of empty calories that's devoid of nutrition and simply fills them up without properly fueling their growth and health.

Here's another problem: inconsistency. You say that you sometimes offer custom meals and sometimes refuse, but truth be told, your children remain consistent—they know if they complain long enough, you'll give in. For things to change, you must be the one who changes.

While it's unlikely there's anything you can do to make your kids suddenly start happily eating anything you put in front of them, you can make some changes to the daily routine to lessen your own stress and get them on the path to being less picky at the table. You can do this by making thoughtful decisions about how mealtime should progress. There is no one right solution here for every family, so I suggest that you first take a quiet moment to reflect on your own needs and goals. Consider how mealtime looks in your household now, and ponder your answers to the following questions:

- What are the biggest things that annoy or distress you?
- What do you do now in response to these things?
- What do you do against your better judgment because you feel pressured?
- What's the worst that can happen if you change your current response? Can you live with that?
- What are you willing to bend on? What issues are non-negotiable?
- What solutions can you apply for each of the problems you've identified?

Keep in mind the old adage that you can lead a horse to water, but you can't make him drink. In the same vein, you can lead your kids to the dinner table, but you can't make them eat. But you can control what food you offer, your own behavior, and your own response to negativity.

Making a plan and then going "cold turkey" on your kids could work, but only if you prepare the new plan in detail and then stick with it no matter what. Here are a few thoughts on making your new meal plan work:

- Make a list of your kids' favorite foods. Figure out how to include a bit of each child's acceptable food on the table each evening. This way you'll be sure to have at least one thing that each child will eat, and it may get them started so that they'll eat the other foods as well. That macaroni and cheese your child loves could be a small side serving to the fish and broccoli.

• Keep meals simple. If you cook elaborate recipes that no one eats, your own wounded feelings will get in the way. You'll feel hurt, and that often leads to anger, which only makes the situation worse.

• Decide in advance how you will handle a noneater. If your child is old enough, is it okay with you if he makes himself a healthy alternative? Is he relegated to available leftovers? Or would you rather he leave the table and have something to eat later?

• Preplan a wholesome snack to occur about an hour after dinner. This is long enough that it doesn't appear you are caving to a picky eater's antidinner whims but not so long that his hunger causes him to have an emotional meltdown.

Take a look at these ideas and the suggestions throughout the rest of this book, then make your plan. It may help to write it down and discuss it with your partner or anyone else who spends time with your children. Having all the adults in your kids' lives on the same page is definitely helpful. Keep in mind that you may have to revise your plan several times as you move along.

Transition from Refined Flour to Whole Grains

I have no idea how it happened, but my kids will eat only white-flour products—bread, pasta, rice, crackers. I eat whole grains, so I can't believe I've let this happen! How do I get them moved over to whole grains?

This is a common dilemma, even for whole-grain-eating parents! Sadly, the majority of grains that children are exposed to in today's world are the refined variety. Whether it's fast-food restaurants,

Wes, four years old

birthday parties, or even Grandma's house, it seems that white flour dominates the offerings. You can't totally control what goes on outside your kitchen, but you can control your home, affect your children's tastes and habits, and increase their whole-grain consumption. Follow some of the ideas mentioned earlier and expanded on here:

• Use the gradual substitution method. For example, when making pasta, begin by replacing one-third of your children's usual choice with whole-grain pasta. Adding a small bit of whole-grain product doesn't change the taste much, so it's likely they won't notice. Over time, increase the percentage, working your way up to 100 percent whole grain. By doing this a bit at a time, you gradually introduce your kids to the flavor and texture of whole grains. This same method works for moving from white rice to more vitamin-filled brown rice.

Use this same substitution idea as a way to wean your children from refined-flour, high-sugar breakfast cereals. Begin by sprinkling in just a little bit of a healthy whole-grain, low-sugar, high-fiber cereal. Gradually increase the amount of healthy cereal until you can serve mainly the healthy choice with just a bit of the sugary stuff sprinkled over the top. Pay attention to the nutrition labels of your kids' cereal choices and pick the healthier options; some contain whole grain, much less sugar, and more fiber than others.

• To switch your children from white bread to whole grain, you'll have more success if you start by using a type of bread with a whole-grain blend or only some added whole grain, since the texture will be similar to that of white bread. When making a sandwich, begin by replacing the bottom slice only with the whole-grain blend piece. After a time, use a grainier whole-grain piece for the bottom and see if you can replace the top piece with the blended style; once they accept that, you can move to two slices of regular whole grain. This may take months, so be patient. Remember that your children are still getting white bread products elsewhere, which can affect how quickly they embrace whole grains. Even if the changeover takes a year, you can affect their choices for the rest of their lives, so this is an endeavor worth pursuing.

• Whenever you prepare soups, stews, stir-fries, or casseroles, add some whole-grain pasta or brown rice to the mixture. It will blend in with the other ingredients and introduce your children to the whole-grain flavor. Use whole-grain bread crumbs in meat loaf, hamburgers, and chicken recipes.

• When baking familiar recipes that use flour, begin to substitute enriched white flour with whole-wheat flour using the same gradual substitution method I mentioned previously. Begin with one-quarter whole-wheat flour; then after a few times, increase the whole wheat to half the recipe, moving toward 100 percent whole wheat.

Don't be fooled by packaging. Many items are labeled with confusing terms that sound like they are whole grain but really aren't. Phrases such as "100 percent wheat," "seven-grain," "bran," "stone-ground," and "multigrain" may refer to an enriched, processed, or minor ingredient. You cannot tell whole grain by color or texture, because added ingredients can make a product look like something it really isn't; for example, added molasses can make a white bread look like a brown whole-grain loaf, but it is really tinted white bread. You can be sure that you have found a genuine whole-grain product when one of the ingredients on the following chart shows up as the *first item* on the label.

Whole Grains

Amaranth	Bulgur	Popcorn	Whole rye
Barley	Couscous	Quinoa	Whole wheat
Brown rice	Millet	Spelt	Whole-grain corn
Buckwheat	Oats	Wheat berries	Wild rice

Use Preferences as Cornerstones

Our son has only four foods that he eats willingly: noodles, bananas, cheese, and sandwiches made with peanut butter and strawberry jam—on white bread only. Any other food requires a battle to get him to eat. He honestly could survive on those items and nothing else!

It's very common for a young child to pick a handful of favorite foods and refuse anything that isn't on his preferred list. To ignore that list and serve other foods instead will likely result in major

Mother-Speak

"When it comes to food, we have always prioritized eating a range of foods and being willing to try something new. It's not easy, and it takes a positive attitude and creativity. We tell our kids that only your tongue can be the judge, because your eyes can trick you into thinking food isn't good. We insist they take a taste of everything and give us a thumbs-up, thumbs-down, or thumbs-medium. We show them that we take their opinion seriously by not forcing them to eat the foods they give a thumbs-down to and encouraging them to give a second try to a thumbs-medium. This process almost always works to encourage them to try new foods."

—**Kristi, mother of eight-year-old Jimmy, five-year-old Mary, and three-year-old Katy**

food battles. A better approach is to figure out how to work with his favorites to create a healthy, well-rounded diet for your child.

If your child is stuck on a food as a staple, try to find ways to make it healthier by choosing a more wholesome version of the same item. As suggested earlier, if PB&J is his food of the moment, buy natural, no-sugar peanut butter; all-fruit jam; and whole-grain bread. Rather than making a total switch that he will likely refuse, make small changes, one piece at a time. To make a step-by-step change for even the pickiest eater, mix half his normal jam with half no-sugar fruit spread, and half the low-sugar peanut butter with his current favorite. Over time, as he becomes accustomed to the taste, increase the amount of the healthier ingredients.

You can also introduce subtle changes to these favorite foods to provide a more varied diet for your child. For instance, sometimes substitute almond butter for the peanut butter, low-sugar peach preserves for the strawberry jam, or a high-fiber English muffin for the white bread. Substitute only one part at a time, though, so you don't create a whole new meal that becomes unacceptable to him.

While a more varied diet is better overall, making your child's regular staples a bit healthier and mixing them up with some new ingredients makes these food jags (eating only a few favorite foods day after day) less of an issue. Try some of the following ideas:

- Consider giving in—a little. Give your child a miniserving of one of his current favorites as a small side dish to the meal. A quarter of a peanut butter and jelly sandwich makes a fine side dish to roasted chicken.
- Add just a few tablespoons of a new food as a side dish to his regular fare.
- Be creative with a new food's presentation, such as serving it on a special plate or using the ingredients to make a food face, while keeping the familiar food boring.
- Don't worry so much about occasional, short-lived food jags; they are normal. Evaluate your child's diet on a weekly, not daily, basis. Most kids, when given nutritious options, will eat a balanced diet when viewed over a week.

Put Vegetables on a Pedestal

I serve vegetables on my kids' plates for every meal, but they'll rarely eat them. I know they don't get enough veggies, but how do I get them to eat the green stuff?

The first step to increasing your children's vegetable consumption is your own attitude. It's an odd fact that while vegetables are a healthy cornerstone of any diet, they are usually relegated to a back-corner side dish. While interesting recipes appear for main

Charlotte, three years old

dishes, vegetables are often steamed or boiled in a routinely boring presentation. They rarely (if ever) get the spotlight. Here are some tips to elevate the status of vegetables in your house:

• When kids ask, "What's for dinner?" we often name the meat and starch ("Chicken and rice" or "Steak and potatoes") and don't even mention the vegetables. Start naming the vegetables first to give them their proper due. If you can create a fun or interesting name for the vegetable of the day, you can help your children view them in a different light. So what's for dinner? "We're having Leaf Us Alone Brussels Sprouts along with chicken and rice." (The recipe for these amazing brussels sprouts appears in Part 4.)

• Go beyond a dab of butter and a dash of salt. Search out new recipes for vegetables (again, see Part 4). Try stir-frying a mix of vegetables with olive oil to give them an attractive presentation and a unique flavor. Add a sprinkling of nuts or seeds or a dribble of sauce. Mix two or even three kinds of vegetables together for a colorful dish.

• It can be fun to serve vegetables in interesting containers or arranged colorfully in patterns or shapes. This creativity can make them more appealing and enticing.

• Serve a platter of raw veggies with a dipping sauce, such as ranch dressing, yogurt, or hummus (see Part 4 for a hummus recipe idea and page 125 for a chart of interesting dips). Kids often prefer raw vegetables to cooked, especially if they can dip them.

• Keep small, interesting containers of chopped vegetables in the refrigerator at child-eye level, and let your kids know they can eat these veggies anytime they want without permission.

• Serve vegetables as an appetizer or a first course, as this is when children are hungriest. The nutritional sciences department at Penn State discovered that when children were given an ounce of carrots (served alone) as the first course of their meal, their

---

Mother-Speak

"Instead of any kind of starchy chips, we make baked kale—for fun, we call them Crazy Kale. I let the kids rip up fresh kale. Spread the pieces in a thin layer across a cookie sheet, spray them lightly with olive oil (don't dribble it as this makes the kale soggy), and sprinkle them with a bit of salt. Bake at 350°F about 10 minutes, or broil for 3 to 5 minutes (watching closely so it doesn't burn). We go through at least two bunches of kale a week with our kids. Even adults, who claim not to like kale, will eat this like popcorn!"

**—Andrea, mother to seven-year-old Tessa, four-
year-old Kieran, and two-year-old Jenson**

vegetable intake for the entire meal rose by nearly 50 percent! The kids not only ate the carrots, but they ate more broccoli too. The researchers don't know why this occurred, but it's definitely a practice worth adopting.

• Routinely serve two vegetables at dinner so you double the chance that your children will eat at least one of them. Plus, getting them accustomed to seeing two vegetables on the table will build an expectation that vegetables are an important part of the meal.

• While you are teaching your children about nutrition in these early years, go ahead and hide some vegetables within other recipes to up their daily quota. It's easy to add chopped spinach to hamburgers, pureed squash to macaroni and cheese, crushed cauliflower to mashed potatoes, or bits of carrots and broccoli to spaghetti sauce. (See the chart on page 75 for specific ideas and the Sneaky Chef recipes in Part 4.)

Make Mealtime More Interesting

My kids are far more interested in playtime than in coming to the table to eat. What can I do to make them interested in eating?

It's true, kids just want to have fun. So why not use this concept to entice them to the table? Many of my test parents report success when getting creative with the presentation or names of the foods they want their kids to eat. You certainly don't have to do this for every food or every meal, but it is a great way to take a bit of stress out of getting your little one to eat.

You can come up with a crazy name for just about any food. Get your children involved in the naming process. Once a food gets

Mother-Speak

"My daughter loves a fun book by Lauren Child called *I Will Never Not Ever Eat a Tomato.* It's a book about Lola, a very fussy eater. One day, after rattling off her long list of despised foods, Lola's older sister, Charlie, has a great idea. She tells Lola that the orange things on the table are not really carrots, but 'orange twiglets from Jupiter,' and the peas are in fact 'green drops from Greenland.' Mashed potatoes, when pitched as 'cloud fluff from the pointiest peak of Mount Fuji' suddenly seem appealing to Lola. And in the end, she even eats moon-squirters (tomatoes, of course)."

—Lisa, mother of eight-year-old Amelia

a fun name, go ahead and call it that whenever it's on the menu. Funny, ironic, or gross names often get the best results. Here are some examples to get you started:

Broccoli—Magic Mini-Trees
Kidney beans—Dinosaur Eggs
Melon balls—Pixie Basketballs
Green beans—Muscle Men
Beef chunks or meatballs—Mighty Meat
Spaghetti—Wiggly Worms
Green olives—Monster Eyes
Celery stick filled with peanut butter and raisins lined up on
    top—Ants on a Log
Raw veggies and dip—Dippity Doo and Veggies Too

Adding your children's names to any food or meal gives them a reason to try it and love it. Experiment with something like these: Sloppy Joans, Ben's Belly-icious Beans, Sophie Soup, or Lillianburgers. Or name food after the dog or your children's favorite cartoon characters.

A great way to get younger children engaged in mealtime is to have the food actually "talk" to them. The spaghetti can call them to the table for dinner. The beans can "ask" to climb into their mouths and visit their tummies. But whenever a food "talks," make sure you use a funny, disguised voice—beans never sound exactly like Mom or Dad, you know.

In addition to fun names, you can make any food more interesting by changing the presentation. Try some of these ideas:

- Use cookie cutters or a knife to make fun shapes out of sandwiches, pancakes, and cheese. Shapes, strips, circles, or funny-shaped bits can be more fun than a plain old square.

- Use a plate as a canvass and arrange the food as a face or in the shape of an animal. You can even let your children build their own creations, then dare them to eat the "nose" or take a bite of the "foot."

- Use anything other than a kitchen plate to serve up food. It's so easy to use colorful containers, toy dishes, an ice cube tray, or a muffin tin as dishes. These options often make a meal or snack more interesting to a child.

Mother-Speak

"I've noticed that if I give my kids a little bit of an assortment of many different things, they eat more overall. One of their favorites is a nibble tray filled with cheese, fruit, cereal, bite-sized muffin pieces, sunflower seeds, sausage, and anything else I have available."

—Sharee, mother of four-year-old Tommy and two-year-old Ben

- Purchase a dinner plate set decorated with your children's current favorite TV or movie characters. Or take them to the store and let them choose their own dishes, even if they don't match your set.
- Get artistic! Your child's plate doesn't always have to look the same, with a pile of each different type of food neatly arranged. Instead of putting food in tidy piles on the plate, make designs, separate the peas all over the place, or string beans or noodles around the edge of the plate. Try alternating veggies, meat, and grain in mini-piles or stripes all over the plate, or combine them to make a pattern or design. While we adults are used to seeing food in tidy arrangements, lots of kids find a fun disarray more appealing. Be imaginative when you're dishing out the next meal and see what happens!
- Combine fun names *and* interesting presentations to make a meal irresistible. Stand up broccoli pieces in a bed of mashed potatoes and sprinkle on bits of meat to make an edible forest. Pick a fun name, such as Dinner Forestville, or name each forest after one of your children. Design a solar system with meatballs, an aquarium with fish sticks, or a zoo out of cut-up sandwich pieces. A boring dinner can become irresistible.
- There's no reason for your children's food to always be boring beige or white. You can use food coloring or brightly colored vegetables or fruits to create pink mashed potatoes (for recipe, see Part 4), purple mashed cauliflower, blue oatmeal, or red yogurt. You can also add color to the water when boiling pasta or potatoes and have green potatoes or orange pasta. Your kids can participate by choosing the colors, chopping the fruits or veggies, or adding the drops.
- Get out the craft supplies and help your kids design and make their own placemats, table centerpiece, or napkin holders. If this project is a hit, make it a monthly routine, perhaps deco-

rating the table for each holiday or season. Once your children have decorated the table, they may be more interested in sitting there.

- Have a formal "taste test" as a great way to clear your refrigerator of the week's leftovers and get your kids to eat. Put out an assortment of foods in small bowls or dishes, and invite everyone to take small tastes of various dishes and comment on their flavors. You can also ask your children to be your official taste-testers when you prepare a meal. Ask formal questions, "Do you think this contains enough pepper, kind sir?" This game can be played over and over!

- Try a different configuration of a regular food. For example, instead of spaghetti with meatballs, serve spaghetti with one mega-meatball in the middle of the plate; or you can make minimeatballs and have lots of them surrounding the spaghetti. Instead of carrots cut in circles, make one long, skinny strip from one end of

Audrey, two-and-a-half years old

the carrot to the other; instead of cutting apple chunks, make long spirals using a potato peeler.

- Kids love foods they can pick up and dip, so anything that comes with a sauce can be served separately with the sauce in a bowl. Here are a few dipping ideas:
  - Fruit in mashed cottage cheese or yogurt
  - Apples in peanut butter
  - Pita bread in hummus (There's a great hummus recipe in Part 4.)
  - Carrots, celery, zucchini, and other veggies in ranch dressing, hummus, or yogurt
  - Chicken pieces or beef cubes in marinara sauce or beef juice
  - Meatballs on toothpicks dipped in mashed potatoes, soup, or marinara sauce

You can find a chart with many dip suggestions on page 125.

- Take a look at how your children's favorite fast food is presented and present their dinner in a similar arrangement. Fold the chicken into a paper wrapper, serve applesauce in a minicup, and stand green beans in a paper cup to achieve an interesting "frenchfryish" appearance.

Mother-Speak

"My daughter likes peas, so anything that looks even a little like a pea gets a new name: soybeans are 'soy peas'; kidney beans are 'red peas'; garbanzo beans are 'bumpy peas.' She will eat anything that's a pea! We are Asian, and we eat a lot of rice, so one of the best ways to get her to eat some is to make it into balls: 'small balls,' 'big balls,' 'squished balls,' or 'flat balls.' She has also started counting the balls, so we line them up and count them too."

—Anusha, mother of seventeen-month-old Vasundhara

Avoid Food Commands

Growing up, we had to eat what was given to us and were always told to clean our plates, even when we hated the food. I always felt that was unfair as a kid, but now I feel like I've gone totally in the opposite direction. My daughter never likes what I serve for dinner, so I always end up making something different for her. Is there a happy medium?

It used to be common to command that children clean their plates at every meal. Several studies on this practice, including those by Brian Wansink, Ph.D., of Cornell University and author of *Mindless Eating*, uncovered that children who were forced to eat everything they were served ate more food than was necessary for their health and then went on to eat twice as much dessert as children who were not required to clean their plates. If children grow up with this rule and continue following it as adults, it puts them at high risk for obesity, since the portion sizes in today's dining world have become excessively large, and teaching a child to clean his plate "could unknowingly be inhibiting the development of the child's self-control around food," says Dr. Wansink. If your child tends to eat everything on her plate, whether because of past rules or habits, then provide her with smaller servings and the invitation to ask for seconds of anything she'd like. This will encourage more thoughtful eating habits.

Conversely, it is important that you don't become a short-order cook who creates a custom meal for your child at every sitting, since over time this process will wear you out and make her an even pickier eater. However, that doesn't mean you have to force her to eat things she really doesn't like. Every person has food preferences, and it's polite to respect those, as long as they aren't

Mother-Speak

"One trick that has worked for us has been to incorporate our daughter's imagination into mealtime. If we are having broccoli for dinner, we say that she is having a 'broccoli party' in her tummy, and each bite of broccoli contributes something to the party (cake, candles, balloons, napkins). Also, I sometimes tell her that the chicken pieces on her plate are lonely, and they would like to join their friends in her tummy. Motivating her through her imagination seems to work wonders! Not that I'm able to (or plan to) do this with every meal, but sometimes it helps to get over the hump if she is hesitant about some food on her plate."

—Mary, mother of three-year-old Annika

excessive and overly restrictive. Here are a few tips that can make your meals a bit more enjoyable for everyone:

• Accept that there are some foods your child simply won't like and allow her to pass on those. Avoid serving them as the main dish, or offer her an alternative when you do. As an example, my oldest daughter detests even the smell of salmon, and she's had this aversion since she was young, so we serve it only when she's not eating with us.

• Make sure at least one item on the menu is something your child likes, but don't have an abundance of this item—just enough for a small serving to whet her appetite and get her to start eating the meal.

• When possible, make use of the previous day's leftovers to offer an alternative choice at a meal. For example, if today's veg-

Shriya, two years old

etable is brussels sprouts, and your daughter hates them, give her the leftover green beans from yesterday's dinner.

• Don't allow your child's pickiness to become a full-blown battle at every meal. This may just reinforce her digging in her heals. Plan ahead to ward off potential issues. Then don't argue over food issues at the table; this just creates a negative cloud over what should be pleasant family time.

Try Family-Style Serving

No matter what I put on my son's plate, he complains. It's too much, the food is "touching," or he doesn't like it. It's a scuffle every time I hand him a plateful of food!

Here's an idea: don't fill his plate! Instead, serve dinner family-style by putting all the food in bowls or platters on the counter or table and allowing your child to fill his own plate. If he's too young to do this himself, let him point and choose as you spoon it out for him, or you can hold the plate while he dishes out his choices.

Of course, you'll have to create a few guidelines—taking a boat load of pasta but no vegetables won't do. You can require that he take a little bit of everything, but let him decide exactly how much and where it sits on the plate.

A fun alternative to try once in a while is to make a "menu" by jotting down the meal choices on a piece of paper and allow your child to check off the things he'd like to eat. It's a great way to rid your refrigerator of leftovers once a week. This idea also provides a fun reading lesson.

Often, if a child has more control about what's on his plate, he'll be more likely to eat it.

Mother-Speak

"If possible, arrange a meal with a child of similar age who has good eating habits. When your child sees another child staying seated for the whole meal and enjoying greens, he is much more likely to do the same thing."

—Cindy, mother of two-year-old Isaac

Let Your Kids Help Prepare the Food

My boys seem not to care about food at all. It isn't important to them, and so they complain when I call them to the table to eat.

It's common for children to be uninterested in food. They're often far more concerned with playing than in having a meal. Unlike adults, they don't view mealtime as a social event, and they don't get great pleasure from a well-crafted meal. Of course, it's important for them to eat, so here are a few tips to get your children more interested in the food that's being served than in finishing their game:

• Get them involved from the start. Ask for their input on your meal plans for the week. Let them help shop and pick the assortment of produce, the type of soup, or the shape of pasta you buy. Let them choose between two options before you start meal

Mother-Speak

"I have one idea that has worked for my very picky toddler, who frequently refuses to eat anything at all. To encourage her to eat, we bring a 'friend' to the table. The favorite doll, stuffed animal, or toy of the day joins us for the meal. We give her little friend a bite, and then my daughter will happily take one next. If she still refuses, we make a big deal about how well the doll is doing and how yummy the food is. Often, she will join in the eating fun. She also loves to feed the doll or feed us bites of food (or pretend bites). Seeing us enjoy her food helps her to enjoy it."

—Lisa, mother of eighteen-month-old Emily

Anneliese, two years old

preparation. If they have a hand in choosing the food, they will probably be more interested in eating it.

• Let your kids help prepare food. Even a three-year-old can spread jam on toast or snap the ends off beans. Older kids love rolling up their sleeves and actually participating in the cooking. Children will be more likely to eat and enjoy the meal when they have had a hand in its preparation.

• You can involve your children in the planning, shopping, and preparation of an entire meal once in a while. Plan this for days when you have extra time. Relax and view it as a bonding activity as much as a kitchen duty. Expect spills, mismeasured ingredients, and the fact that everything will take three times as long with their "help." It's all worth it, though, when you see the joy on their faces as they eat their meal with enthusiasm and glow with pride at your compliments.

• Get creative with your eating location, and your children may become more interested in mealtime. Have a picnic on the family room floor, sit outside on the porch or deck, or have a car party in the driveway. One of my test moms reported serving lunch to her toddler in the (dry) bathtub just for fun, and a test dad told of having a picnic with his kids *under* the dining room table.

• Grow a few tomato plants or herbs on your windowsill. If you want to and have a place to do it, plant a whole vegetable garden and some strawberry plants. Let each of your children "adopt" a plant or two as their own and let them do the watering and weeding. Kids love growing their own food, so it becomes a fun science project as much as a tactic to encourage them to eat more vegetables and fruit.

Zachary and Christian, five years old

Create Mealtime Routines

Dinner around our house is sporadic, changing almost daily based on our busy schedule with three kids. Sometimes we eat dinner at the table together, but usually it's kind of a free-for-all—everyone grabbing something and eating on the run. Would it be worth it to make more of an effort to have a daily family dinner together?

It's absolutely, totally worth the effort! There are lots of great reasons for a family to eat dinner together, especially when it's a busy family like yours. Many studies have been done on the ritual of a family dinner, and here are some of the advantages that have been uncovered:

• Families who routinely eat dinner together eat more whole grains, vegetables, and fruits than those whose members eat on their own. A planned sit-down event reaps a healthier diet for all.

• Children who eat with the family are more adventurous with food, probably because they see others eating different things.

• Family mealtime may be a key to a better future for your children in many ways. Kids who grow up with this routine are less likely to have eating disorders and more likely to eat a balanced diet. Children who sit at the table daily with their parents are less likely to experiment with smoking, drinking, or drugs; less likely to suffer from depression; and more likely to be better students. *The Journal of Adolescent Health* even reported that teenagers who ate meals with their family on a regular basis engaged in less sexual activity than teens who didn't sit down to family meals. A study by Boston College showed that teenagers who share regular time with their families have closer relationships with their parents, which leads to more conversation and better decision making.

Professional-Speak

"Oprah Winfrey conducted a Family Dinner Experiment. Five families volunteered to accept the challenge to eat dinner together every night for a month, staying at the table for a half hour each time. As part of the experiment, all family members kept journals to record their feelings about the experience. At first, sharing meals was a chore for many families, and the minutes at the table dragged on. But by the end of the month, the families were happy and planned to continue dining together most evenings, if not every night. When the families appeared on the *Oprah Winfrey Show* at the end of the experiment, the greatest surprise to the parents was how much their children treasured the dependable time with their parents at the table."

—**Martha Marino, M.A., R.D., C.D., and**

Sue Butkus, Ph.D., R.D., Washington State University

If a family dinner custom is new to your household you may want to consider these tips to ease everyone into a fresh and rewarding routine:

- Begin by picking just one or two nights for family dinner, and aim to build the schedule from there. Choose less hectic days when everyone is home at the same time.
- Eat early enough so that everyone isn't hungry beforehand and filling up on snacks, but not so late so that people are starving and grumpy.
- Choose meals that everyone likes, or at least have one food on the table that each person enjoys.
- Include dessert after dinner, but here's the secret—make it a small serving so that it's just a bit of sweetness and not enough to cause your children to pass on dinner foods so they can "save

room" for dessert every night. In addition, don't make sugary dessert a part of every dinner; your children will come to expect it. Instead, alternate sweet treats with fruit, frozen yogurt, or cheese as the dessert offering.

• Make mealtime long enough but not too long. Lingering can bring boredom or fussing.

• Carefully guide the conversation so that it's lighthearted and enjoyable. Steer away from any negatives, even those pertaining to mealtime manners. Until the routine is in place, you want every dinner hour to be a happy experience.

• Encourage everyone to be there for your regular family dinners, but don't be forceful or demanding. If someone has a work, school, sports, or music conflict, simply gather everyone else together on that day.

• If one parent's work schedule conflicts with an early, child-friendly dinner hour, then work around it. You might eat the meal early and then save dessert for when the parent arrives, or you may want to shelve the idea of a family dinner in favor of a family breakfast. At a minimum, gather everyone together for a meal on nonworkdays and find other times to spend as a group, such as taking a walk, sharing a board game, or playing yard games outside.

Get a Sleepyhead to Eat a Good Breakfast

My daughter wakes up slowly and has no appetite first thing in the morning. She has a big lunch, so is there any reason to push breakfast?

Actually, there are some very important reasons for your child to have breakfast. Depending on when she had dinner or an evening snack, by the time breakfast time rolls around, she may not have had anything to eat for as much as twelve to eighteen hours. If she does not "break her fast," then her morning hunger cue might shut off entirely, fooling her into thinking that she's not hungry.

If your child takes a long time to get hungry and eats an hour or more after waking, she'll get into that habit. Keeping a late breakfast routine day after day resets her hunger clock so that she won't be thinking of eating in the morning at all. Because this early nutrition is critically important to her health and well-being, you will need to be her morning hunger clock until she develops a new pattern.

A child who isn't in the mood for breakfast will likely reject a big meal, so don't try to convince her to eat one. Instead, present this as more of a morning snack and provide something light, such as a breakfast smoothie made of yogurt, milk, and fruit; toast with peanut butter; or a parfait made of yogurt, fruit, and granola. Think outside the box, as some children will be more interested in nonbreakfast foods such as pasta, rice, or even a sandwich in the morning. A more creative menu will likely be more acceptable to a child who isn't feeling very hungry. Provide this "morning snack" at the exact same time after she wakes each morning—such as fifteen to twenty minutes after she gets up. If you stick to this schedule, her system will adjust, and she'll begin to expect something to eat at that time each day.

Offer Snacks—but Make Them Healthy Ones

Every time I walk into the kitchen, my preschooler is digging in the pantry for a snack. He fills up on crackers, chips, and cookies and then turns his nose up at dinner!

Snacks are important for a young child, since it's hard for that little tummy to go for long periods without nourishment. The real issue here is that your child is snacking on the wrong types of food between meals. This problem is both easy to solve and a huge challenge. The simple answer is to restock your pantry. You can also put a time limit on snacking—stop the snacks in the hour or two before dinner. Limit the number of high-fat and high-sugar foods sitting on the shelves that are available to your child, and shut the door during your predinner prep time. Snacking can be a good thing, but only if it consists of healthy foods and is timed so that it doesn't interfere with your child's regular meals.

The biggest challenge here is that you'll have to take a good look at what and when you are eating too. To convince your child to snack on carrots and apples and not to nibble before dinner, you'll need to show the way.

If your child is truly hungry while you're preparing a meal, it's a good idea to set out an "appetizer" of raw vegetables with dip, apple pieces, or a cup of soup to tide him over until mealtime.

If he is hungry halfway between meals, he definitely should have a snack, but make it a nourishing one. It can help reduce complaints, if you choose a substitute snack that is similar to your child's original choice. Use these suggestions to switch him from a less desirable food to a healthier choice:

If your child likes this:	Try this healthier alternative:
French fries	Baked sweet potato fries or butternut squash fries
Pizza	Whole-wheat English muffin or flatbread topped with pizza sauce, low-fat mozzarella cheese, minced vegetables, and ground turkey
Ice cream	Sorbet, fruit ice, partially frozen yogurt, or frozen fruit such as bananas or cut grapes (These can be a choking hazard, so use caution.)

(continued)

If your child likes this:	Try this healthier alternative:
Jelly beans or gummy candy	Dried fruit, fruit leather, or fruit roll-ups (Watch the sugar content.)
Milkshakes	Homemade smoothie with low-fat milk, yogurt, fresh fruit, and ice; or frozen bananas and strawberries blended with soymilk or almond milk
Potato chips	Baked pita chips, whole-wheat pretzels, baked kale (see page 97 for recipe), or popcorn (This is not for babies or young toddlers, as it can be a choking hazard.)
Cookies	Graham crackers, fig bars, or homemade cookies baked from healthy ingredients
Crackers	Toasted breadsticks; baked tortilla pieces; whole-grain, low-sugar cereal

Try, Try, and Try Again

Is it true that a child has to be exposed to a new food many times before accepting it? If so, what's the best way to get my picky eater to try new things?

Yes, it's true! A picky eater often has to be exposed to a new food ten to fifteen times before even tasting it. Children trust familiar things in their lives and are often suspicious of something

Mother-Speak

"To introduce my kids to some new foods, I create a food treasure hunt. I have the kids play in their room so I can put out the food and make a map to each place with clues to the next food spot. They don't get the next clue unless they try the food at each spot. I try to have only two new or not-so-keen-on foods along with about three things they do like along the way. The treasure at the end is dessert!"

—**Melissa, mother of five-year-old Brenna,**
four-year-old Gianni, two-year-old Giulio,
and nine-month-old Brydie

new and different—this applies to food too. A food that has an unusual appearance, color, smell, or texture can be off-putting to a young child. That's why repeated exposure helps. Eventually the unusual food becomes familiar, and at that point, the child becomes open to the idea of tasting it and giving it a fair evaluation.

Knowing these facts gives us insight into how to introduce new foods and what to expect when we do. Here are a few tips:

- Begin by putting a tiny bit of the new food—such as two chickpeas or one brussels sprout—on your child's plate along with regular favorites. Don't expect him to eat it, and don't make a comment if he pulls it apart, smells it, or smashes it. Allow the experimentation to occur—it's the first step to acceptance. If you've displayed the new food on your child's plate eight to ten times and he still hasn't eaten any, then gently encourage him to take "just one bite."

- Pick one or two new foods at a time and put one on your child's plate three or four times per week for several months. When he sees it enough times he'll eventually give it a taste.
- Let your child observe you eating the new food. Mention to your spouse or a friend that you enjoy the food so that your child hears your comment. Studies tell us that when children are certain their parents or other important people in their lives really like a food (not just eat it out of duty, but actually *enjoy* it), they decide it's a good thing to try for themselves.
- If you are eating with another adult, offer that person a taste of the new food. Ask her in advance to try it willingly and declare it tasty. When a child sees someone else being adventurous, he may be more willing to do so himself.
- After your child has tried the food and found it at least minimally acceptable (meaning he doesn't spit it out or gag on it), try putting it out as an appetizer before dinner is served. If your child is hungry, and it's the first thing offered, he may actually eat a bite or two.

Mother-Speak

"I put kale on his plate and put kale on his plate and put kale on his plate. My son tried it and grimaced, and we praised him for trying it. Pages flew off the calendar, and his beard grew down to the floor, and *then* one day he ate it without comment. And then one day he ate it and said, 'This is actually not as bad as I thought.' After which a pair of bluebirds draped the banner of joy around my shoulders."

—Catherine, mother to eight-year-old Ben
and four-year-old Birdy

Faeryn, three years old

Monitor a Balanced Diet by the Week

Overall, my daughter eats a fairly balanced diet, but some days she seems to hardly eat at all. These low-food days really have me worried.

It's perfectly normal for your child to be hungrier on some days than others. Many different things can affect her need for food. On days when she's more active, she may naturally be hungrier; on the other hand, she could be so busy that she forgets to eat. Some days she may be eating more calorie-rich or fiber-heavy foods that fill her up so that she seems to be eating less. Also, growth in the toddler and preschool years is uneven, alternating between spurts and plateaus, and your child's need for food will change along with this growth pattern.

Your overall goal is to feed your child a balanced diet every day and to offer a well-rounded, healthy assortment of foods for breakfast, lunch, dinner, and snacks. That's the *goal*. The reality is that you won't be able to guarantee that your child eats what is offered, you can't possibly monitor every morsel she takes in, and her food needs may be slightly different each day. It may be more practical to monitor her diet over the course of a week. When you look at your child's diet this way, you may be surprised how well balanced it is over a longer time frame.

Customize a Daily Meal and Snack Schedule

I always try to serve three meals plus two snacks. On many days, my son has a good breakfast and lunch and several snacks throughout the day, but by dinnertime, he's not interested in eating much food. Should I change our routine and skip a snack to stretch more time between meals?

Since your son is eating well for two meals plus several snacks, it's likely he's getting all the food he needs when he needs it. I would not try to "stretch" him between meals, as he's likely eating more during the active part of his day and winding down his eating along with his activity level. It's common for young children to have two bigger meals and then two or three smaller snacks.

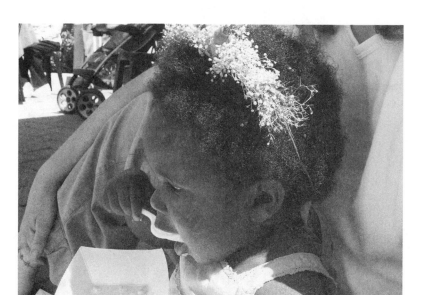

Alexandra, three years old, with Mum Susan

What's important is that your child isn't going more than two or three hours without some nutrition and that his daily calorie intake meets his physical and mental needs. The idea of three meals plus two snacks is only a guideline, and what some children eat looks more like two meals plus three snacks, or even one meal plus four snacks. As long as his overall diet is well-rounded, and he has plenty of energy, it's likely his schedule works for him.

If, however, you find that his energy level lags at the dinner hour, and he exhibits more whining and tantrums at that time, then it's a sign he needs either more naptime or more dinner. Experiment with his nap schedule to be sure he has an adequate midday sleep. Experiment also with serving some simple dinner foods that he'll find easy to eat, and serve them almost as a snack rather than a meal. Easy foods such as oatmeal and fruit, toast and cheese, or yogurt and granola might be good choices for a light evening choice.

Keep Realistic Expectations

There is no way to get our toddler to sit down for a whole meal. He is happy for about ten minutes, then he loses interest and wanders off, or he fusses if we make him stay at the table.

Wow! You can get your toddler to sit at the table for ten whole minutes. Congratulations—that's a long time for a little guy. This is the age when the dinner table isn't much fun, and a child's appetite and serving sizes are minuscule. Demanding that a toddler stay at the table until his parents are done eating is asking for an unpleasant experience for everyone. A better choice is to modify your expectations and enjoy your toddler's limited interest; after ten minutes, as soon as he's done eating, allow him to get down and play while you finish your meal without the distraction and disruption of battling him to stay seated. As he gets older, you can expect him to sit at the dinner table longer.

At this point, you want to begin to build a routine of family mealtime, not expect perfection. Here are a few tips:

• Put your child at the table only when all the food has been served and his plate is sitting at his place, ready to eat. Adding any extra time up-front while you dish things out is wasting valuable sitting time.

- Give your child a smaller plate and provide just a petite serving of each type of food. Spread the food out in small piles so the meal won't appear daunting.
- Be sure you are providing your child with meals plus snacks throughout the day. As a matter of fact, you might view this as five or six minimeals that break up the day's nutritional goals into manageable pieces.
- If your toddler resists mealtime, try giving him a different chair. If he's still in a high chair, try a booster seat on a regular chair, or put a small table (like a child's plastic picnic table) next to the adult table. A new and interesting arrangement might be better suited to his desires.
- To keep your child sitting at the table and enjoying it, include him in the conversation. Typically, if the adults are talking and the child is quietly listening, he'll lose interest. However, if he's being included, he'll be more interested in staying put.
- If you'd like your child to learn to stay at the table until everyone is done eating, that's a fine thing for him to learn. However, once he's actually done eating, remove his place setting and give him a toy to play with or crayons and paper to color with. That way, he'll get used to the dinner table routine, but you won't be forcing him to eat more than he needs or permitting him to get bored and fussy.

Allow Some Grazing—with Guidelines

Our twins don't eat much at meals, but they get enough calories by grazing on snacks throughout the day. I've heard that grazing is good. Is it?

If your children's grazing routine means they eat wholesome foods five or six times a day, then yes, grazing is fine. However, too many children today spend a big part of their day snacking on crackers, cereal bits, cookies, cheese, and juice. This isn't a healthy pattern for a number of reasons.

The first problem with snack grazing is that children take in a majority of their calories with foods that have low nutritional value. Snack foods that are popular with young children tend to be high in carbohydrates. Kids who fill up on them tend to keep hunger too much at bay, so they never have the slightest feeling of hunger. This means they'll happily snack on tasty treats but turn up their noses at a dinner plate. And forget the idea of getting a picky eater to even try a new food when hunger isn't a motivator.

This kind of continual daily grazing also plays havoc with a child's digestive system, which is constantly trying to keep up with an influx of food without a break. The digestive system functions best when it has some time to process a meal or snack before moving on to the next one.

Another problem with continuous grazing is that it leads to unconscious eating. Children who are used to snacking while sitting in the car, watching television, reading, or just passing the time aren't making food decisions based on hunger or the need to eat; rather, they're just in the habit of snacking.

Semigrazing—eating three meals plus two or three healthy snacks, all of which take place with a few hours of digestion in between—is the best solution for your children's eating schedule.

Kids who love to graze will often enjoy a meal that is served in a more casual way. When you serve fruit, vegetables, bread, crackers, pancakes, or meat along with a pile of toothpicks and a bowl of dipping sauce it's likely your picky eater will dig right in! See Part 4 for dip recipes or try some of these options:

Dip	Dippers
Cottage cheese—mashed or blended—with different additions, such as lemon juice, sweet chili sauce, mashed pineapple, or yogurt	Vegetable sticks (carrots, celery, peppers, zucchini, cucumber, tomato) or rice crackers
Greek yogurt with minced herbs or finely diced sweet onion or cucumber	Vegetables, pita, toast, chicken pieces, or baked potato wedges
Peanut butter blended with vanilla yogurt	Apples, bananas, pears, crackers, pita bread pieces, or celery
Canned black beans blended with a clove of garlic, a squeeze of fresh lime, and cumin	Baked tortilla pieces or baked potato wedges
Plain yogurt mixed with a package of dry vegetable soup mix, chopped parsley, and finely grated cucumber	Vegetables, pita bread pieces, potato wedges, or beef chunks
Silken tofu blended with dry vegetable soup mix, minced onion, parsley, or pureed vegetables and spices	Vegetables, potato wedges, or meat chunks
Sour cream, parsley, lemon juice, and chopped chives or onion	Beef cubes, chicken pieces, pork strips, broccoli, cauliflower
Pizza sauce, shredded mozzarella cheese, grated parmesan cheese, and minced basil	Bread pieces, whole-wheat pizza crust in strips, beef cubes, or chicken strips
Bouillon broth made with water, bouillon powder, finely minced onion, garlic, celery, and carrots	Beef, pork, or chicken
Strawberry yogurt mixed with whipped cream or Jell-O	Mixed fruit pieces

Monitor and Limit Juice Consumption

Is it okay for all of a toddler's daily servings of fruit to be in the form of juice? Mine loves juice but doesn't eat much whole fruit.

Many children love juice. The beverage is often served in easy-to-carry containers or bottles and can be refilled frequently on request. It often becomes more about the comfort action of sipping than the need for quenching thirst. There are several problems with this all-day, juice-on-demand routine.

A picky eater may get too many of his daily calories from his juice drinks, meaning he fills up on juice and then gets fewer nutri-

Zaara, two-and-a-half years old

ents from other foods that it displaces. In addition, juice often replaces milk, which results in a shortage of important calcium.

Excess juice consumption throughout the day takes away the feeling of hunger, which is appropriate for mealtime. A child who is slightly hungry before a meal and fills up with an appetizer of juice comes to the table lacking the desire to eat, making his picky eating habits even worse.

It's wise to adhere to the American Academy of Pediatrics' recommendation to limit juice to four to six ounces a day for children one to six years old, and eight to twelve ounces for older kids. I also recommend that juice be served after the meal instead of before or along with the food, so that it doesn't interfere with a balanced diet.

Be Tricky . . . with an Agenda

I bought some new cookbooks that show how to hide vegetables in my child's favorite foods. But I'm wondering if being "sneaky" is a good solution?

There are some tremendous recipes that include hidden vegetables and proteins in tasty, less-nutritious foods that children gravitate toward. (You can find a sampling of these recipes in Part 4.) This is a terrific way to fill the vegetable voids that occur in your child's diet.

An important key to creating lifelong healthy eating habits is patience, and there will be many times when your picky eater is working harder to avoid good foods than you are trying to get them eaten. It is during these times that being sneaky will pay off, since your child will ingest those valuable nutrients but be unaware of it.

Over time, after she has enjoyed lasagna boosted with spinach and blueberries a few times, you can let her in on the secret by inviting her to help prepare the dinner. You can matter-of-factly include these ingredients—let her puree the spinach or mash the blueberries. This way she'll learn that she can enjoy healthy food too.

During the picky eating phase, you can use the sneaky method liberally, while at the same time continuing all your other strategies to broaden your child's acceptable food list.

Be the Example

> My husband is a picky eater and is far too vocal about his own preferences. The minute he announces that he hates beets, I know my kids won't go near them. Is he making them picky with his own habits?

Daddy isn't *making* your kids picky (they can mange that quite nicely on their own), but his actions can definitely reinforce their pickiness and steer them away from even trying foods that he doesn't like but they may—if they ever taste them. He's also demonstrating the kind of manners and lack of food acceptance that they'll come to accept as normal. Children learn what they live, and this applies to mealtime behaviors.

Several studies have shown that children are more likely to try a new food—and enjoy it—if they see their parents or other caregivers showing enthusiasm for it. The studies pointed out that it's more than seeing someone eat the food; the kids have to be convinced that the person likes it. So ask your husband to please quiet down about his food dislikes for your children's sake, and next time you dig into a big plate of veggies, announce, "Yum, yum. This sure is delicious!"

Eating Away from Home at Restaurants

My husband and I like to go out to eat and bring the family, but our kids are so picky about their food that it's always a disaster. They don't want to try anything new, and they never actually eat what we order. Is there any way to improve our family restaurant experience?

Adults go out to restaurants to enjoy the food, the environment, the social experience, and a night off from cooking and cleaning. Children haven't matured to that level and would likely not choose to go to a restaurant unless it's a child-centered, fast-food extravaganza.

What parents often fail to understand is that children who are picky eaters at home will be even pickier at a restaurant. Even food that sounds familiar can turn out to be something totally different than they expect. For example, the grilled cheese sandwiches your children order may turn out to be Havarti on sourdough, which may not look or taste anything like what you serve at home.

View your restaurant meals as a social event rather than a food event, if that's really why you're going out. Choose restaurants that offer at least a few of your children's acceptable food choices, and order something that has a fighting chance of being eaten. Try to choose foods that are prepared simply, without extra ingredients, and ask for sauce or topping on the side. Ask questions about how the food is prepared, and request modifications if possible. Keep in mind that even then, the food may be just different enough that it won't pass muster. It's important that you don't require your children to eat everything they're served, especially since restaurant serving sizes tend to be excessively large. It should be a normal process to box up the leftovers and take them home. This is actually a good habit, since it teaches your children not to overeat when they're out.

What to Do About a Slow Eater

My son is the slowest eater on the planet! We're nearly late for preschool every morning because he lingers at the breakfast table. It takes him an hour to nibble on a snack. And he's the last one eating dinner when everyone else is gone and I'm cleaning the kitchen. How can I speed him up?

The real question here is, *should* you speed him up? To answer this, you need to figure out why your little one eats slowly, how this affects his food intake, and if he is getting all the calories and nutrition he needs for the day.

Slow eating, in and of itself, is not a bad thing—actually it's a good thing. Several studies, including those reported in the *American Journal of Clinical Nutrition* and the *British Medical Journal*, report that eating slowly allows for more enjoyment of a meal and gives more time for the body's fullness signals to work properly. A lifetime of slow eating lowers the odds of a person becoming overweight. These studies mention that it's a good idea to start mellow eating habits in childhood.

So slow eating, as a practice of enjoying food and respecting the body's signals, is a positive practice. However, many children eat slowly for reasons that aren't so constructive, so it's best to watch your child to determine why he does it.

Some kids are slow eaters because they aren't hungry when they are required to eat a meal. They pick at their food, mash it, and shove it around on their plate. In essence, they are being pushed into eating more food than their body needs, and dawdling is their way of preventing overeating. You can determine if this is the case for your child by reviewing the appropriate food serving charts in Part 2. The solution here may be an adjustment of meal times or a reduction of serving sizes.

Another reason children eat slowly is that they fill up on the liquids that are served right before or along with their meal. Milk, juice, and even water can fill children up so they no longer feel hungry and pick at their food. This can be solved by serving the beverage at the end of a meal.

Other children are slow eaters because they are distracted from eating. Watching TV, playing with toys at the table, even engaging in storytelling or interesting conversation becomes the highlight of their time at the table, and the food takes a backseat. In this case, eliminate outside distractions: shut off the TV, and make sure your child isn't a chatterbox who dominates the conversation, leaving him little time for eating.

In a few rare cases, a child eats slowly because undiagnosed food sensitivities are bothering his stomach and interfering with proper digestion. Some children will approach foods with different textures in various ways. Take note if your child eats at a normal pace for certain foods, but a slower pace for others; this may be a clue to specific food-related problems.

Some children eat at a normal pace but slow to a crawl once they are no longer hungry. Watch to see if your child begins a meal with gusto and then begins to pick and play. When he loses speed and interest, it's time to allow him to be excused from the table.

If your child is a slow eater because he savors his meals, try to find ways to allow him the time he desires to eat. This might mean getting up fifteen minutes earlier in the morning or slowing down the dinnertime rush. It can also be smart to serve the healthiest foods as the first course to be sure he eats them and save the less nutritious choices for afterward.

If your child is a healthy weight, has lots of energy, and is healthy, then he's probably getting exactly what he needs from the foods he eats, and his slow pace is comfortable for him.

Serve Milk: A Nutrient-Dense Beverage

Does milk really build strong bones and teeth? My mom always made us drink milk, but should I make my children drink it as well? Should I serve them whole milk, low-fat, or nonfat? What about chocolate milk; is that a good option?

Once a child passes her first birthday and is weaned or weaning off breast milk or formula, milk is still the recommended beverage for a healthy, balanced diet. At this time, the U.S. Department of Agriculture, Canada's Food Guide, and other nutritional experts suggest that young children have two cups of milk, or the dairy equivalent, each day, divided into three or more servings. According to the American Academy of Pediatrics, children from one to two years old can drink whole milk (3.5–4 percent fat), unless there is a family history of heart disease, high cholesterol, or obesity, or the children themselves are overweight (a body mass index in roughly the ninety-fifth percentile or above). In such cases, a child should be given reduced-fat (2 percent) milk. After age two, the experts say that all children should switch to low-fat (1 percent) milk and milk products.

Milk is considered a nutrient-dense food, since it is the source of a varied and important mix of vitamins and minerals essential

Nikhil and Aria, two years old

for the growth of more than just bones and teeth. Its calcium, protein, vitamin D, and other nutrients are an excellent way to fuel children's fast-pace growth and are necessary for the development of muscles and nerves. These nutrients are available in other foods, of course, such as fish, fruits, and vegetables, but it's common for children to be lacking in the proper mix and serving sizes of these foods, so milk—a drink often popular with even the pickiest eaters—can fill the gaps.

It's best to offer children unflavored milk, but some don't care for it. In that case, offer yogurt or cheese instead. It's also acceptable to offer flavored milk. It's best to purchase low-sugar flavored milks or flavor the milk yourself so you can control the added sugar. Chocolate, while popular, isn't the only flavor available. You can blend fruit, such as berries, or vanilla or almond extract into milk for a sweet flavor. Even when you're unable to monitor the sugar content, such as the chocolate milk offered at day care or school, it's fine to permit your children to drink flavored milk, if the alternative is drinking none at all, since flavored milk contains all the nutrients of plain milk. This advice stems from a study done by the Prime Consulting Group that studied the milk-drinking habits of children from fifty-eight schools where flavored milk was discontinued from the lunch offering. Researchers learned that when denied the flavored milk, 35–50 percent of the children (numbers varied by school) chose to drink no milk at all. Further, the researchers saw an overall decline in nutrients when the kids missed their milk at lunch, since they did not make up the missed nutrients with other menu choices.

Children who have a mild degree of lactose intolerance are often able to accept small servings of milk without incident. However, if a child has a more intense intolerance, and dairy products bring on such problems as stomachache, vomiting, gassiness, or eczema, you'll need to find ways to be sure she eats a balanced diet that contains plenty of calcium, vitamin D, and protein. These nutrients can be found in fortified soy or rice milk, dark green vegetables, fish, tofu, beans, and fortified orange juice (in limited quantities).

Research is pointing the way toward the use of milk obtained from grass-fed cows as being more healthful than the commonly sold milk from grain-fed cows. Do your research, and check with your health care provider to determine if you should be providing your children with organic milk from grass-fed cows. Avoid raw milk; always purchase pasteurized milk, because pasteurization kills potentially dangerous bacteria.

Don't Limit Your Kids to Kid Food

At what age should I upgrade my toddler from chicken nuggets to real chicken and from macaroni and cheese to pasta marinara?

In a perfect world, you'd never have to upgrade your toddler from kid food to adult food, because he'd eat adult food from the start. Real chicken is far superior to processed nuggets, and homemade pasta can be infinitely healthier than boxed convenience foods. If, however, your child is already hooked on the kid version of typical foods, you can begin to wean him from these by serving half-and-half meals: a few nuggets plus a few pieces of chicken cut in nugget-sized pieces, for example. You can also search out recipes for making healthier versions of your child's favorites, such as pizza with whole-grain crust, low-fat cheese, and turkey sausage. (Check out the recipes in Part 4 for ideas.)

Supplement with Vitamins if Necessary

I'm working on getting my picky eater to expand his diet, but in the meantime, I worry that he's not getting the nutrients he needs every day.

If your child doesn't eat enough, doesn't eat frequently enough, or avoids entire food groups such as vegetables, milk, or proteins, it would be wise to talk to your health care provider about giving him a multivitamin to round out his nutritional needs during these important growth years.

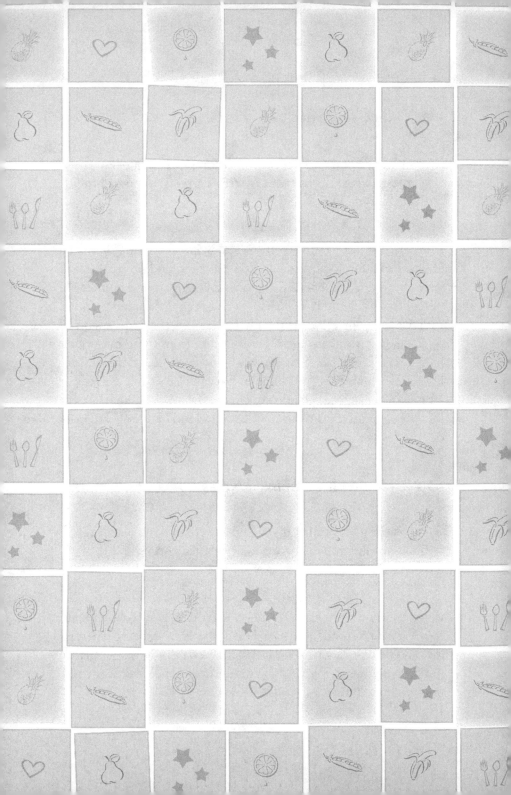

4

The Experts' Favorites

·················

Recipes Even Your Picky Eater Will Love

Now you have an assortment of tips and solutions to convince your picky eater to change her choosy ways. I realized that it would be much easier for you to apply all these ideas if you had recipes for foods that are enticing and delicious. So I pulled together a group of well-known, inspiring family cookbook authors and asked if they would each provide a few recipes to get you started on your recipe collection. They were excited to share some of their favorites.

Your child might not be a fan of a green pile of spinach, but when it's an ingredient in Lord of the Apple Rings, Grow-a-Garden Dip, or Mexican Lasagna, you might just find him asking for more. And when that spinach is a hidden surprise in the Brainy Brownies you serve for dessert, you can feel really good about your nonvegetable-eating picky eater actually meeting the recommended daily amount of vegetables.

I think you'll love the great recipe names too—what child would turn down at least a taste of Leaf Us Alone Brussels Sprouts, Treasure Triangles, or Smiley Face Casserole? And when Pink Potatoes hit the table, I'm willing to bet that your child will be the first to dig in.

Miles, three years old, and Sol, two years old

Here you'll find many creative and tasty ways to prepare and serve the healthy foods you really want to be part of your child's everyday diet. So pick something good and give it a try!

Bon appétit!

Fabulous Fried Rice

From *The Sneaky Chef,* by Missy Chase Lapine

Makes 8 servings

2 tablespoons (30 mL)
   canola, vegetable, or
   olive oil
3 large eggs
½ cup (118 mL) White
   Puree (recipe follows)
1 small onion, minced or
   pureed
1 to 2 cloves garlic,
   minced
2 teaspoons (4 g) fresh
   ginger, minced (or
   ⅛ teaspoon [.25 g]
   ground ginger)
2 cups cubed chicken,

ham, pork, beef, or shrimp, cooked (approximately
   12 ounces [336 g]), optional
4 cups (700 g) cooked rice, cold (ideally brown rice)
2 tablespoons (30 mL) low-sodium soy sauce
Salt and freshly ground black pepper to taste
Optional extra boost: ½ cup peas (80 g) and/or
   2 scallions, diced

Heat 1 tablespoon (15 mL) of the oil in a large nonstick skillet
or wok over medium heat. In a large mixing bowl, whisk the eggs
with the White Puree. Add the egg mixture to the skillet and
scramble quickly until almost set, then transfer the eggs back to
the bowl.

Increase the heat to medium high and heat the remaining oil. Add the onion, garlic, and ginger and stir-fry for about 2 minutes. Add more oil, if needed. Add the cubed meat or shrimp, and stir-fry for another 2 minutes. Add the rice and soy sauce; toss until the ingredients are combined well and the rice is heated through. Allow the rice to brown in the skillet before stirring in the egg mixture. If using, add the peas and scallion for the last minute of cooking. Season with salt and freshly ground pepper to taste.

Sneaky Chef Make-Ahead Recipe: White Puree

From *The Sneaky Chef*, by Missy Chase Lapine

Makes about 2 cups

2 cups (200 g) cauliflower florets (about ½ a small head)
2 small to medium zucchini, peeled and coarsely chopped
1 teaspoon (5 mL) fresh lemon juice
1 to 2 tablespoons (15–30 mL) water, if necessary

To prepare the cauliflower on the stovetop, pour about 2 inches (5 cm) of water into a pot with a tight-fitting lid. Put a vegetable steamer basket into the pot, add the cauliflower, and steam for about 10 minutes, until very tender. Drain.

To prepare the cauliflower in the microwave, place the florets in a microwave-safe bowl, cover them with water, and microwave on High for 8 to 10 minutes, or until very tender. Drain.

Meanwhile, place the zucchini and lemon juice in a food processor and pulse a few times. Add the cooked cauliflower and 1 tablespoon (15 mL) of the water (work in batches if necessary) and puree on High until smooth. Stop occasionally to push the contents to the bottom with a spatula. If necessary, use another tablespoon of water to make a smooth puree, but the less water, the better.

This recipe makes about 2 cups of puree; double it if you want to store more. It will keep in the refrigerator for up to three days, or you can freeze ¼-cup portions in sealed plastic bags or small plastic containers.

Sneaky Chef Brainy Brownies

From *The Sneaky Chef*, by Missy Chase Lapine

Makes about 30 small brownies

6 tablespoons (85 g) unsalted butter

¾ cup (135 g) semisweet chocolate chips

2 large eggs

2 teaspoons (10 mL) pure vanilla extract

½ cup (100 g) sugar

½ cup (118 mL) Purple Puree (recipe follows)

¼ cup plus 2 tablespoons (47 g) all-purpose flour
    (or half whole-grain pastry flour and half white flour)

¼ cup (24 g) oat bran

1 tablespoon (5 g) unsweetened cocoa powder

¼ teaspoon (1.5 g) salt

Preheat the oven to 350°F (177°C). Butter or spray the bottom only of an 8-inch (20-cm) or 9-inch square (22.5-cm) baking pan.

Melt the butter and chocolate chips together in a double boiler or metal bowl over simmering water (or in the microwave on High, checking every 15 seconds). Remove from the heat and allow the mixture to cool a bit. Meanwhile, in another bowl, stir together the eggs, vanilla, sugar, and Purple Puree. Combine this purple egg mixture with the cooled chocolate.

In a mixing bowl, stir together the flour, oat bran, cocoa powder, and salt. Add this to the chocolate mixture and blend thoroughly, then pour the batter into the baking pan.

Bake for 30 to 35 minutes, until a toothpick comes out clean. Allow the brownies to cool completely in the pan before cutting them, and use a plastic or butter knife for easier cutting. Dust them with powdered sugar before serving.

They keep for a week in the refrigerator, tightly covered.

Sneaky Chef Make-Ahead Recipe: Purple Puree

From *The Sneaky Chef,* by Missy Chase Lapine

Makes about 1 cup

3 cups (90 g) raw baby spinach leaves*
1½ cups (222 g) fresh or frozen blueberries, no syrup or
  sugar added
½ teaspoon (2 mL) lemon juice
1 to 2 tablespoons (15–30 mL) water

Rinse the spinach well, even if the package says it's prewashed. If you're using frozen blueberries, give them a quick rinse under cold water to thaw them a little, then drain.

Place the spinach in the food processor and pulse a few times; this will reduce the amount significantly. Add the blueberries, lemon juice, and 1 tablespoon (15 mL) of the water; puree on High until the mixture is as smooth as possible. Stop occasionally to push the contents to the bottom with a spatula. If necessary, use another tablespoon of water to create a smooth puree.

This recipe makes about 1 cup of puree; double it if you want to store another cup. It will keep in the refrigerator up to three days, or you can freeze ¼-cup portions in sealed plastic bags or small plastic containers.

---

* Note: it is essential to use raw baby spinach for this recipe.

Starry Night Stew

From *The Toddler Café*, by Jennifer Carden

Makes 3 servings

1 15-ounce (425-g) can black beans, drained
    (may be low or reduced sodium)
1 cup (176 g) frozen sweet potato chunks, thawed
¼ cup (59 mL) chicken broth or vegetable broth
    (may be low or reduced sodium)
¼ cup (59 mL) fresh orange juice
2 tablespoons (15 g) tiny star pasta or ditalini
¾ teaspoon (4.5 g) kosher salt
Zest from half an orange, optional

Put the beans, sweet potatoes, broth, and orange juice into a saucepan and bring the mixture to a boil over medium-high heat.

Take the pan off the heat and, using a hand blender, puree the soup in the pan briefly, about 3 seconds, to break up any big chunks of sweet potato. If you don't have a hand blender, mash the chunks with a fork or potato masher.

Bring the stew back to boil, add the pasta and salt, and simmer about 8 minutes, or until the pasta is soft. Take it off the heat and add the orange zest, if using.

Variation

You can use any kind of bean for this recipe; experiment with different flavors. (White beans make a good option.)

Tips

- Search out new selections in the pasta aisle; there are lots of tiny pastas and rice that you may never have noticed.
- For a fun way to serve this dish, cut an orange in half, scoop out the flesh, and fill it with stew.
- Sprinkle shredded cheese or diced avocado on top.

Treasure Triangles

From *The Toddler Café*, by Jennifer Carden

Makes 36 triangles

2 tablespoons butter (29 g) or 1 tablespoon vegetable oil
    (15 mL)
2 bananas, sliced in rounds
¼ cup (40 g) diced onion
1 15-ounce (425-g) can black beans, drained
½ teaspoon (3 g) kosher salt
1 16-ounce (454-g) package frozen puff pastry, 2 sheets
1 cup (113 g) shredded Monterey Jack or mild cheddar cheese
Egg wash: 1 egg beaten with 1 tablespoon (15 mL) water

Heat the butter or oil in a medium sauté pan over high heat. Add the bananas and sauté until golden. Remove the bananas to a bowl.

Add the onion to the sauté pan and cook for 3 to 5 minutes, until clear and softened. Add to the bananas.

Add the beans to the bowl. Using the back of a fork or a potato masher, mash the bean mixture to a coarse paste; season with the salt and cool.

Preheat the oven to 425°F (218°C). Line a baking sheet with parchment paper or spray it with cooking spray.

Unfold each puff pastry sheet on a lightly floured cutting board. Cut each piece into nine equal squares. Place 1 heaping table-spoon (8 g) of cheese in the center of each square. Place 1 table-spoon (11 g) of the bean mixture on top of the cheese.

Fold one corner of the dough over the filling to the opposite corner, forming a triangle. Using a fork, seal the edges of the dough. Arrange the triangles on a rimmed baking sheet; brush with the egg wash. Bake the triangles for about 20 minutes, until golden brown and puffed.

Variations

See what you have on hand. Try pinto beans and corn or cooked crumbled bacon and a dot of peanut butter instead of the black beans and onions.

Tips

- Tell your kids these are treasure triangles and have them guess what the flavors are.
- Puff pastry is located in the freezer section of your grocery store with the frozen piecrust.

- Put the finished raw triangles in the freezer for 5 minutes before cooking. The colder the dough, the more beautiful the finished product.
- Filled unbaked triangles can be stored in the freezer for up to two months. To bake frozen triangles, follow cooking instructions, adding ten minutes to the cooking time.

Lord of the Apple Rings

From *The Toddler Café*, by Jennifer Carden

Makes about 6 servings

Olive oil spray or butter

½ cup (54 g) dried bread crumbs or hazelnut meal (see Tips)

4 ounces (112 g) raw bulk chicken-apple sausage (see Tips)

¼ cup (39 g) frozen spinach, thawed and drained

1 egg, beaten

1 Granny Smith apple, cored and sliced into ¼-inch (0.6-cm)
    rings

Ground cinnamon, for dusting

Preheat the oven to 375°F (191°C).

Line a rimmed baking sheet with aluminum foil or parchment paper, and spray with cooking spray or brush with butter. Set aside.

Mix together the bread crumbs, sausage, spinach, and egg in a medium bowl. Set aside.

There should be a hole in the center of each apple ring. Place the rings on the baking sheet and spray or brush each with oil or butter. Using a small cookie scoop or teaspoon, make 1-inch (2.5-cm) balls of the meat mixture and place one in the center of each apple ring. Bake for 20 minutes, or until the meatballs are firm to the touch.

Place on a plate, dust with cinnamon, and serve.

Variations

If you are crunched for time, use canned pineapple rings in water instead of apple slices. Dry them off with a paper towel before cooking, then follow the same procedure as described. Pineapples and apples can also be grilled before filling for a different and delicious flavor.

Tips

- Add plain yogurt as a sauce. Ask your kids to stack the rings in a tower and see how high they can go; everything that falls has to be eaten.
- Nut meal is simply finely ground nuts, and some grocery and health food stores sell it. To make your own, grind nuts in a food processor, stirring frequently to loosen the clumps. Store in an airtight container in the refrigerator or freezer. (Do not make this recipe with nut meal if any child who may eat it has nut allergies.)
- If you can't find bulk sausage, just remove the casings from uncooked link sausage.

Leaf Us Alone Brussels Sprouts

From *Petit Appetit: Eat, Drink, and Be Merry*, by Lisa Barnes

Makes 6 servings

1 pound (454 g) brussels
    sprouts
¼ cup (59 mL) extra-virgin
    olive oil
1 teaspoon (5 mL) freshly
    squeezed lemon juice
⅛ teaspoon (.75 g) salt
⅛ teaspoon (.25 g) freshly
    ground black pepper

Preheat the oven to 375°F (191°C). Line a jelly roll pan or shallow baking pan with aluminum foil.

Cut off the bottom stem or core of each sprout. Carefully peel away the leaves until it becomes too hard to peel. Cut off the bottom core again and peel more layers. Continue cutting and peeling until it is too difficult to peel apart. (Have your children help with the peeling. Instruct them to pass you the sprouts as they get too tough to peel, then cut the cores and give them back for further peeling.)

Place the leaves in a large mixing bowl. Drizzle with olive oil and lemon juice; stir until all the leaves are coated. Sprinkle with salt and pepper and stir again.

Spread the leaves on the prepared baking pan in a single layer. Bake for 10 to 12 minutes, until the leaves are cooked and start to crisp, turning golden around the edges.

Happy Hummus

From *The Petit Appetit Cookbook*, by Lisa Barnes

Makes 2⅓ cups

2 cups (328 g) cooked
   or canned organic
   chickpeas/garbanzo
   beans (may be low or
   reduced sodium)
⅓ cup (80 g) tahini
   (sesame seed paste)
1 large clove garlic,
   minced (optional)
Juice of 1 organic lemon
2 tablespoons (30 mL)
   extra-virgin olive oil,
   divided
½ teaspoon (1.5 g) ground
   cumin

If using canned chickpeas, drain and rinse them thoroughly until the water is clear. Process the chickpeas, tahini, garlic, lemon juice, 1 tablespoon (15 mL) of the oil, and cumin in a food processor or blender until pureed. Scrape down the sides of the bowl and add the remaining tablespoon of oil. Process for 20 to 30 seconds for a pastelike consistency, or longer for a smoother texture. Add more oil or lemon juice to taste.

Tip

Some people call the main ingredient in this recipe *chickpeas*, while others refer to them as *garbanzo beans*. Either way, they are a great source of protein for the whole family. Hummus makes a terrific dip with vegetables, as well as an alternative spread for sandwiches, bagels, and toast.

Out of the Garden Pancakes

From *The Petit Appetit Cookbook*, by Lisa Barnes

Makes 8 to 10 4-inch pancakes

1 cup (71 g) organic broccoli florets

12 organic asparagus spears

1 cup (6 ounces [170 g]) sliced organic mushrooms

¼ cup (40 g) chopped organic onion

1 large garlic clove, minced

¼ cup (59 mL) expeller pressed canola oil

⅔ cup (83 g) organic whole-wheat flour

1 tablespoon (3 g) chopped fresh dill

⅛ teaspoon (.75 g) sea salt

1 large cage-free, organic egg

¼ cup (59 mL) organic milk

1 cup (113 g) shredded cheddar cheese

Place the broccoli and asparagus in a steamer basket set in a pot filled with about 1 to 2 inches (2.5–5 cm) of lightly boiling water. Do not let the water touch the vegetables. Cover and steam for 4 to 5 minutes, or until tender.

Put the steamed vegetables, mushrooms, onions, and garlic in a food processor and pulse on and off to chop, or you can finely chop them by hand. Be careful not to puree. Transfer the chopped ingredients to a large bowl and mix in the oil, flour, dill, and salt with a rubber spatula or wooden spoon. Stir in the egg and milk until combined.

Coat a large nonstick skillet with cooking spray and place over medium heat. Drop the batter into the skillet, using ¼ cup (59 mL) for each pancake, and cook until firm on the bottom, about 2 minutes. Turn the pancakes with a spatula and sprinkle the cooked side with cheddar cheese. Cook the other side until golden, about 1 minute.

Tip

You can use this recipe to make adult hors d'oeuvres for your next gathering. Drop the batter by the tablespoonful to create a single-bite treat.

Grow-a-Garden Dip

From *Green Princess Cookbook*, by Barbara Beery

Makes about 4 cups

½ cup (115 g) organic sour cream
½ cup (118 mL) organic plain yogurt
2 tablespoons (8 g) chopped organic flat-leaf parsley
2 tablespoons (12 g) chopped organic green onion tops
1 teaspoon (3 g) organic garlic powder
½ teaspoon (1 g) organic paprika
½ teaspoon (3 g) all-natural sea salt
¼ teaspoon (.5 g) organic black pepper

10 ounces (280 g) organic frozen chopped spinach, thawed and
    squeezed dry
1 organic avocado, peeled, pitted, and chopped
½ cup (75 g) diced organic red bell pepper

Garnish
1 organic tomato, chopped
¼ cup (20 g) shredded organic Parmesan cheese

Combine the sour cream, yogurt, parsley, green onion, garlic powder, paprika, salt, and black pepper in a mixing bowl. Add the spinach, avocado, and red bell pepper. Stir well to blend.

Cover the dip and chill in the refrigerator for 30 minutes or longer before serving.

Garnish with the chopped tomato and shredded Parmesan cheese.

Sweet Potato Veggie Nachos
From *Green Princess Cookbook*, by Barbara Beery

Makes 4 servings

1 medium organic sweet
   potato, peeled and
   sliced into thin rounds
1 tablespoon (15 mL)
   organic canola oil
½ teaspoon (3 g) all-
   natural sea salt
½ teaspoon (1 g) organic
   paprika
½ teaspoon (1.5 g) organic
   ground cumin
½ cup (57 g) shredded
   organic Monterey Jack
   cheese
1 cup (180 g) assorted
   chopped organic
   tomatoes, bell peppers,
   and green onions
1 serrano or jalapeño
   pepper, chopped
   (optional)

Garnish
¼ cup (58 g) organic sour cream
1 tablespoon (1 g) chopped organic cilantro

Preheat the oven to 450°F (233°C). Line a cookie sheet with a Silpat, unbleached parchment paper, or reused clean brown paper grocery bag cut to fit. Spray with cooking spray and set aside.

Place the cut potatoes on the prepared cookie sheet. Pour the oil and sprinkle the salt, paprika, and cumin evenly over the potatoes. Toss them with your hands to coat all sides of the potatoes.

Arrange them in a single layer and bake for 25 minutes, or until the rounds are almost tender.

Remove from the oven and top with the cheese and chopped veggies. Return the cookie sheet to the oven and bake for 5 to 7 minutes, or until the cheese has melted. Remove from the oven, garnish, and serve immediately.

Pizza in My Pocket

From *Batter Up Kids Sensational Snacks*, by Barbara Beery

Makes 2 servings

½ cup (57 g) grated mozzarella cheese
½ cup (57 g) grated provolone cheese
½ cup (118 mL) pizza sauce or spaghetti sauce
¼ teaspoon (1.5 g) salt
Dash of black pepper
2 6-inch (15-cm) whole-wheat pita pockets
Sliced bell peppers, onions, mushrooms, or broccoli
    (optional)
4 pieces of foil (about 8 inches [20 cm] square each)

Preheat the oven to 375°F (191°C). Cut each pita pocket in half with kitchen scissors.

Combine the cheeses in a mixing bowl. Add the pizza sauce, salt, and pepper. Stir to blend all ingredients.

Take a pita pocket in your hand and rest the uncut side on a square of foil. The opening should be facing the ceiling. Spoon a fourth of the cheese mixture inside. Repeat for the remaining pitas.

If using veggies, place them equally on top of the cheese mixture in the four pockets.

Wrap the pitas individually in the foil squares and seal shut. Gently shake each one to spread the filling inside.

Place the foil-wrapped pita-pocket pizzas on a cookie sheet and bake for 8 to 10 minutes, or until cheese is melted. Carefully remove from the cookie sheet and cool 2 to 3 minutes before unsealing.

Tip

Serve these pitas with ranch dressing, hummus, or extra pizza sauce for dipping.

Best Ever Granola

From *So Easy Toddler Food,* by Joan Ahlers and
Cheryl Tallman

Makes 14 to 16 toddler-size servings, or 6 to 8 adult-size servings

4 cups (624 g) old-fashioned oats
1 cup (28 g) Cheerios
½ cup (60 g) chopped pecans or almonds
½ cup (110 g) packed brown sugar
½ teaspoon (3 g) salt
½ teaspoon (1 g) cinnamon
¼ cup (59 mL) vegetable oil
¼ cup (59 mL) honey or maple syrup
1 teaspoon (5 mL) vanilla
1 cup (145 g) raisins or dried cranberries

Preheat the oven to 300°F (150°C).

In a large bowl, mix the oats, Cheerios, nuts, brown sugar, salt, and cinnamon. In a saucepan, warm the oil and honey. Stir in the vanilla. Carefully pour the liquid over the oat mixture. Stir gently with a wooden spoon until the mixture is evenly coated.

Spread the granola on a large (15″ × 10″ × 1″ [37.5 cm × 25 cm × 2.5 cm]) cookie sheet. Bake for 40 minutes, stirring carefully every 10 minutes. Remove from the oven and cool completely. Stir in the raisins or dried cranberries.

Store in an airtight container at room temperature for one week or in the freezer for three months.

Tip

Add this granola to yogurt and bananas or other fruit.

Broccoli and Rice Casserole

From *So Easy Toddler Food*, by Joan Ahlers and
Cheryl Tallman

Makes 8 to 10 toddler-size servings, or 4 adult-size servings

1 12-ounce (336-g) package frozen broccoli, chopped
¾ cup (177 mL) vegetable or chicken stock
1 tablespoon (15 mL) olive oil
1 tablespoon (15 mL) lemon juice
1 teaspoon (6 g) salt
2 to 3 cups (525–700 g) cooked brown or white rice
½ cup (118 mL) milk
½ cup (57 g) shredded cheddar cheese

Preheat the oven to 350°F (177°C).

Prepare the chopped broccoli according to the package directions. Place the cooked broccoli, stock, oil, lemon juice, and salt in a blender and process to a smooth puree. Place the rice, milk, and cheese in an oven-proof casserole dish. Pour the broccoli mixture over the rice and cheese. Toss the mixture gently to blend the ingredients. Place in the oven for 15 minutes, or until it is heated through and the cheese is melted.

Tips
- Make this a one-dish meal. Add 1½ cups (approximately 252 g) diced, cooked chicken when you place the rice and cheese in the casserole dish.
- Serve this as a side dish with hamburgers and whole-wheat buns.

Pink Potatoes

From *So Easy Toddler Food,* by Joan Ahlers and
Cheryl Tallman

Makes 10 to 12 toddler-size servings, or 4 adult-size servings

3 medium-sized white potatoes
1 medium-sized sweet potato
5 garlic cloves, peeled
1 14-ounce (414-mL) can chicken broth
4 tablespoons (57 g) butter or margarine
Salt and pepper to taste

Scrub, peel, and cut the potatoes into 2-inch (5-cm) chunks. Place the potatoes and garlic cloves in a saucepan with the chicken broth. Add enough water to cover the potatoes. Set the pan over high heat and bring to a boil. Boil for 10 to 12 minutes, until a fork slides easily through the potatoes. Drain the potatoes, reserving ¾ cup (177 mL) of the cooking liquid. Mash the cooked potatoes with a potato masher until they are the same color throughout. Stir in the butter or margarine. Add the reserved cooking liquid ¼ cup (59 mL) at a time, until the potatoes are a creamy, whipped consistency. Add salt and pepper to taste.

Tip
Serve with baked chicken, gravy, and steamed broccoli.

Mexican Lasagna

From *Welcoming Kitchen*, by Kim Lutz with
Megan Hart, M.S., R.D.

Makes 6 large servings

2 scant cups (350 g) short-grain brown rice
4 cups (944 mL) water
1 bunch spinach (approximately ½ pound [224 g])
1 tablespoon (15 mL) olive oil
1 garlic clove, minced
1 cup (160 g) chopped red onion
1 cup (136 g) corn, either fresh or frozen
1 4-ounce (112-g) can diced mild green chilies, drained
3 cups (707 mL) tomato sauce, divided
1 cup (236 mL) salsa

2 cups (480 g) refried beans or 1 15-ounce (425-g) can (may be
low or reduced sodium)
12 corn tortillas
½ cup (57 g) shredded cheddar cheese or vegan cheddar
cheese (optional)

Preheat oven to 375°F (191°C).

Combine the brown rice and water in a medium saucepan. Bring to a boil, cover, and simmer over low heat for 40 minutes.

Finely chop the spinach (if using a food processor, add a little water to make a paste).

While the rice is cooking, heat the olive oil in a medium skillet. Sauté the garlic. Add the red onion, corn, and chilies; cook until the onion is soft.

When the rice is finished cooking, stir in the chopped spinach, sautéed vegetables, and 1 cup (236 mL) of the tomato sauce.

Combine the remaining tomato sauce and salsa.

Spread a layer of salsa mixture on the bottom of a 9-inch (22.5-cm) square baking pan. Top with a layer of tortillas. Spread the beans on the tortillas. Top with rice. Repeat layers of salsa mixture, tortillas, beans, and rice. Finish with a layer of salsa. (Optional: Top lasagna with ½ cup [57 g] shredded cheddar cheese or vegan cheddar cheese.)

Bake uncovered for 45 minutes. Lasagna is done when it's bubbly and heated through.

Autumn Spice Pumpkin Muffins

From *Welcoming Kitchen*, by Kim Lutz with
Megan Hart, M.S., R.D.

Makes 12 muffins

2¼ cups (313 g) oat flour
2¼ teaspoons (10.5 g)
   baking powder,
   divided
¾ teaspoon (4.5 g) salt
1½ teaspoons (3 g)
   cinnamon
½ teaspoon (1 g) nutmeg
¾ cup (191 g)
   applesauce
¼ cup (59 mL) canola oil
1 cup (220 g) packed
   dark brown sugar
1 teaspoon (5 mL) vanilla
1 15-ounce (425-g)
   can solid-packed
   pumpkin
½ cup (61 g) dried
   sweetened
   cranberries (optional)

Preheat the oven to 350°F (177°C). Oil a standard muffin pan.

In a small bowl, combine the flour, 1½ (7 g) teaspoons baking powder, salt, cinnamon, and nutmeg. Set aside.

In a large bowl, combine the applesauce and ¾ (3.5 g) teaspoon of the baking powder. Add the oil, brown sugar, vanilla, and pumpkin.

Add the dry ingredients to the pumpkin mixture, one half at a time. Stir to combine. Stir in the cranberries, if using.

Spoon the batter into the muffin pan. Bake for 18 to 23 minutes, or until a toothpick inserted in the center of a muffin comes out clean. Remove from the pan; cool on a rack.

Fruity Chicken Kebabs

From *No Whine with Dinner*, by Liz Weiss, M.S., R.D., and Janice Newell Bissex, M.S., R.D.

Makes 4 servings

8 ounces (224 g) lower-sodium deli chicken or turkey, sliced
   ¾-inch (2-cm) thick
16 green grapes
12 strawberries, cut in half lengthwise
8 8-inch (20-cm) wooden skewers or toothpicks

Cut the chicken into ¾-inch (2-cm) cubes. To make the kebabs, thread 3 pieces of cubed chicken, 2 grapes, and 3 strawberry halves onto each skewer in any order you and your children choose. Be sure to leave enough space at the bottom so that the kids can hold the skewers comfortably.

To wrap for school lunch, lay two skewers on a sheet of aluminum foil and fold the foil loosely over the kebabs.

Tips
- Pack two kebabs with an all-natural fruit smoothie and a mini whole-wheat bagel with light cream cheese to round out a school lunch.
- For younger kids (or those prone to swordfights with skewers), you can cut the ingredients into smaller pieces and serve them with toothpicks instead.

Cheesy Spinach Bake

From *No Whine with Dinner,* by Liz Weiss, M.S., R.D., and Janice Newell Bissex, M.S., R.D.

Makes 8 servings

1 10-ounce (280-g) box frozen chopped spinach, thawed
2 large eggs
½ cup (118 mL) low-fat (1%) milk
1 tablespoon (15 mL) extra-virgin olive oil or melted butter
½ cup (54 g) Italian-style seasoned bread crumbs
½ teaspoon (2.5 g) baking powder
1 cup (4 ounces [113 g]) shredded reduced-fat cheddar cheese
¼ cup (25 g) grated Parmesan cheese
Kosher salt

Preheat the oven to 350°F (177°C). Lightly oil or coat an 8-inch (20-cm) square baking pan or dish with nonstick cooking spray and set aside.

Drain the spinach well by pressing in a colander with the back of a large spoon and using paper towels to remove excess moisture. Set aside.

In a large bowl, whisk together the eggs, milk, and olive oil until combined. Whisk in the bread crumbs and baking powder. Stir in the spinach, cheddar cheese, and Parmesan cheese until well combined.

Spread the mixture evenly in the prepared pan. Bake for 25 to 30 minutes, until the mixture is set and the top is golden brown. Slice into 2″ × 4″ (5-cm × 10-cm) rectangles and serve. Sprinkle the top with a few pinches of salt to taste.

Smiley Face Casserole

From *No Whine with Dinner,* by Liz Weiss, M.S., R.D., and
Janice Newell Bissex, M.S., R.D.

Makes 10 servings

1 26-ounce (737-g) bag frozen smiley face potato fries
1 tablespoon (15 mL) canola oil
8 ounces (224 g) mushrooms, coarsely chopped
1 pound (454 g) lean ground beef or turkey (90% lean or higher)
1 large carrot, peeled and shredded (about 1 cup [122 g])
½ teaspoon (1.5 g) garlic powder
½ teaspoon (.5 g) black pepper
Kosher salt
1 10¾-ounce (301-mL) can lower-fat, lower-sodium cream of
     mushroom soup
1 10¾-ounce (301-mL) can filled with low-fat (1%) milk
2 cups (8 ounces [226 g]) shredded reduced-fat cheddar
     cheese, divided

Preheat the oven and bake the fries according to package directions. When done, remove from the oven and set aside.

While the fries are cooking, heat the oil in a large Dutch oven or saucepan over medium-high heat. Add the mushrooms and cook, stirring frequently, until softened, about 5 minutes.

Add the meat, carrot, garlic powder, and pepper; cook, breaking up the large pieces, until the meat is no longer pink and the carrot is tender, about 5 minutes. Drain the excess fat and season with salt and additional pepper to taste.

Stir in the soup, milk, and 1½ cups (169 g) of the cheese (the mixture will seem very thin at this point, but don't worry). Heat, stirring frequently, until the mixture comes to a simmer. Remove from the heat.

Set the oven to 425°F (218°C). Arrange half the cooked fries in a 9″ × 13″ (22.5-cm × 32.5-cm) baking pan or dish. Top with the meat mixture, the remaining ½ cup (57 g) of cheese, and the remaining potato smiles. Cover loosely with aluminum foil, and bake until the mixture is bubbly, about 10 minutes.

Credits

Recipes from Missy Chase Lapine

From *The Sneaky Chef: Simple Strategies for Hiding Healthy Foods in Kids' Favorite Meals.* Text and photographs © 2007–2010 by Missy Chase Lapine. Used with permission from Running Press. Visit http://www.TheSneakyChef.com.

Recipes from Jennifer Carden

From *The Toddler Café: Fast, Healthy, and Fun Ways to Feed Even the Pickiest Eater.* Text © 2008 by Jennifer Carden. Photographs © 2008 by Matthew Carden. Used with permission from Hi A LLC, Chronicle Books, San Francisco. Visit http://www .ChronicleBooks.com or http://www.jennifercarden.com.

Recipes from Lisa Barnes

Adapted from *The Petit Appetit Cookbook: Easy, Organic Recipes to Nurture Your Baby and Toddler.* Text © 2005 by Lisa Barnes, Berkley Publishing Group, a division of Penguin Group (USA). And *Petit Appetit: Eat, Drink, and Be Merry: Easy, Organic Snacks, Beverages, and Party Foods for Kids of All Ages.* Text © 2005 by Lisa Barnes, Perigee Books, an imprint of Penguin Group (USA). Photographs © 2009 by Lisa Barnes. Used with permission from the author. Visit http://www.petitappetit.com.

Recipes from Barbara Beery

Adapted from *Green Princess Cookbook: Sweets and Treats to Save the Planet*. Text and photographs © 2008 by Barbara Beery, Gibbs Smith. And *Batter Up Kids Sensational Snacks*. Text and photographs © 2005 by Barbara Berry, Gibbs Smith. Used with permission from the author. Visit http://www.kidscookaustin.com or http://www.kidscookingshop.com.

Recipes from Joan Ahlers and Cheryl Tallman

Adapted from *So Easy Toddler Food*. Text and photographs © 2009 by Joan Ahlers and Cheryl Tallman; Fresh Baby LLC. Used with permission from the authors. Visit http://www.freshbaby.com.

Recipes from Kim Lutz and Megan Hart

Adapted from *Welcoming Kitchen: 200 Delicious Allergen & Gluten-Free Vegan Recipes*. Text and photographs © 2011 by Kim Lutz with Megan Hart, M.S., R.D.; Sterling Publishing. Used with permission from the authors. Visit http://www.welcomingkitchen.com.

Recipes from Liz Weiss and Janice Newell Bissex

Adapted from *No Whine with Dinner: 150 Healthy, Kid-Tested Recipes from The Meal Makeover Moms*. Text and photographs © 2011 by Liz Weiss, M.S., R.D., and Janice Newell Bissex, M.S., R.D.; M3 Press. Used with permission from the authors. Visit http://meal makeovermoms.com.

Index

Page numbers in **boldface** indicate recipes.

About the Author

Parenting educator Elizabeth Pantley is president of Better Beginnings, Inc., a family resource and education company. She is a regular radio-show guest and is frequently quoted as a parenting expert in newspapers and magazines worldwide and on thousands of parent-directed websites. She publishes newsletters that are distributed in schools, daycares, medical offices, child-birth-educator programs, lactation centers, doula and midwife offices, and parent programs everywhere.

Elizabeth is the author of eleven popular parenting books, available in twenty-six languages, including the bestselling *No-Cry Solution* series. She was also a contributing author to *The Successful Child* with Dr. William and Martha Sears.

Elizabeth and her husband, Robert, are the parents of four children: Angela, Vanessa, David, and Coleton. Elizabeth is an involved participant in her children's school and sports activities and has served in positions as varied as softball coach, educational board member, and school PTA president.

For more information, excerpts, parenting articles, and contests visit the author's website at http://www.nocrysolution.com.